CW00493590

The Hatfield, Luton and Dunstable Railway
(and on to Leighton Buzzard)
by
Sue and Geoff Woodward

LONDON & NORTH EASTERN RAILWAY
THE LONDON & NORTH EASTERN RAILWAY
COMPANY HEREBY GIVE NOTICE
PURSUANT TO THE PROVISIONS OF THE
L & N.E. RLY ACT 1924 (SECTION 70)
THAT THIS FOOTPATH IS THEIR PRIVATE
PROPERTY.   O.3.

THE OAKWOOD PRESS

© 1994 Sue and Geoff Woodward and Oakwood Press

ISBN 0 85361 469 5

Typeset by Oakwood Graphics.
Printed by Alpha Print (Oxford) Ltd, Witney, Oxon

All rights reserved. No part of this book may be reproduced or transmitted in any form or by any means, electronic or mechanical, including photocopying, recording or by any information storage and retrieval system, without permission from the Publisher in writing.

A general view of Luton Hoo (foreground) and Chiltern Green stations, 1959. Note the old style traffic sign for the level crossing. *A. Willmott*

Published by
The OAKWOOD PRESS
P.O.Box 122, Headington, Oxford.

Contents

Market Day in Luton's Market Square, c. 1908.   T. Hobbs

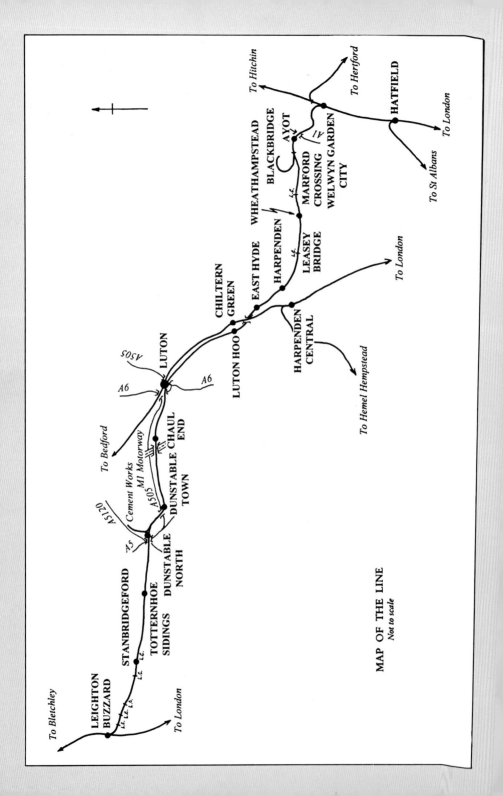

MAP OF THE LINE
Not to scale

Introduction

Towards the middle of the 19th century numerous proposals for railways were put forward, many using parts of previously rejected plans, but in some cases based on completely new plans. One of the earliest planned links between London and Bedford was the scheme of George Remmington in 1836, which would have formed part of a line from London to Manchester. It was to have run from Kings Cross through Barnet, Wheathampstead, Harpenden and Luton, then on to Bedford and Leicester to join the Midland Counties Railway. The Bill for the direct London to Manchester link was considered and rejected by Parliament in 1846.

Again as part of a major route, this time London to Birmingham, a spur line was proposed in 1845 by Robert Stephenson which passed through Luton to Dunstable. It would have taken an almost identical route to the line which was later built, except that from Luton West it would have run to a terminus just below the Union Chapel in Castle Street. This scheme never reached beyond the planning stage, neither did Joseph Locke's proposal of the same year. He, though, was planning a route between Oxford and Cambridge, which would have incorporated a section from Leighton (Buzzard) to Dunstable - by the route later followed. It would then have crossed the A505 road at its present junction with the M1 Motorway and run parallel with the Dunstable Road into Luton, where he planned for it to cross the Moor (a source of trouble to later railway planners!) and over Stopsley Common. A 330 yds-long tunnel was envisaged under the ridge just before Lilley village, from where it would have run on to Hitchin and Cambridge.

The following year saw yet another plan for a line from London to Luton and Dunstable - to be called the Hatfield, St Albans, Luton & Dunstable Railway. This would have left the Great Northern main line at Hatfield station, turned sharply westwards towards Chantry Green and on through Roe Green, Pope's Field, to Beaumonts at St Albans, where it turned sharp right to take it over Dellfield, Bernards Heath to Sparrowswick, Hatching Green, Mutton End and across the A6 (A1081) just south of Roundwood Lane, Harpenden, by a bridge 15 ft high. It would then have crossed the field to the south of Cooters End House and on to Thrales End where a 616 yds-long tunnel under the ridge took it on to New Mill End. From there the line entered Luton via St Anne's Hill and followed the route of the line later built to Dunstable.

In 1847 the London & North Western Railway Company gained powers to build a line frum Watford, via St Albans, Redbourn, New Mill End and Luton, to Dunstable, where it would have joined its branch from Leighton. Agreement was reached between the London & North Western and Great Northern companies that the latter would drop its 1846 proposal for a Luton line, provided it had running powers to Luton over the section from St Albans (in the event of the Great Northern Company building the section from Hatfield to St Albans). In fact this section was built and opened on the 16th October, 1865, but due to lack of funds the London & North Western Company could not proceed with its planned extension and powers lapsed. However, these were renewed on the 4th August, 1853, but only in respect of the Watford to St Albans section, and this opened on the 5th May, 1858.

A plan of 1865 to provide a link between the London & North Western at Hemel Hempstead and either the Midland extension or the Great Northern at Harpenden was rejected by Parliament, but a variation of this scheme was successful in 1866. It took another Act before a line from Hemel Hempstead to Harpenden was built, however. This passed through Redbourn (by a similar route to the previous plan) but then took a northerly route around Harpenden, through Roundwood, crossing the A6 by a bridge before joining the Midland line near Westfields. Known locally as 'The Nickey Line' (many theories have been voiced as to the origin of the nickname), it opened on the 16th July,1877. It did not connect with the LNWR, at Hemel Hempstead, and no further mention was made of a connection with the Great Northern at Harpenden.

It must by now be apparent to the reader that during those early years of railway growth so many proposals were put forward they could not all gain approval and reach reality. One is forced to ask, therefore, how and why those which were built gained the support and permission of Parliament.

The two branch lines about which this book is written were once just proposals, but they were built. Particular accent is put on the Hatfield to Luton and Dunstable branch in an effort to understand its significance in those early days, but no less importance is attached to the Dunstable to Leighton Buzzard branch.

Perhaps the following piece of modern poetry will set the scene and whet the reader's appetite:

> This is the story of a small branch line -
> Insignificant among the complex network
> Of main lines, branch lines,
> Privately owned, narrow gauge and industrial lines.
>
> Why then should its tale be told?
> This is why -
> Its dawning was stormy,
> Its opening exciting,
> Its development uncertain,
> Its closure, perhaps, unnecessary.
>
> Many people worked for it and,
> In turn, it worked for many people -
> The daily workmen and the casual passengers,

The wealthy and the famous.

It served industry,
And even in time of war
It was called upon to play a useful part.
Now it has gone!
How will it be remembered?
And by whom?

This book is written to answer both questions ....

A turn of the century view of Station Road, Wheathampstead.   *Eric Brandreth*

A superb view of the northern end of Hatfield station, c. 1895 with an up express, headed by a GNR, 4-2-2, No. 2 passing at speed. The train has 6-wheel coaches and a 12-wheel dining car in its stock. Luton and St Albans branch lines are on the left. Note the signalling.

E.J. Bedford, courtesy National Railway Museum

Chapter One

History

By the early 19th century, Luton was developing its industry and satisfactory methods of transport were urgently needed. In 1810 a direct stagecoach service started between Luton and London (the journey taking nine hours), whilst Luton industrialists were forced to travel by horse and cart to Leighton (later Leighton Buzzard) to collect their coal supplies from narrow-boats on the Grand Junction Canal. Dunstable was sited on a very busy coach route, with up to 80 passing through the town each day. Thomas Telford dug the cutting through the chalk-hill just north of the town to assist this traffic.

Although horse and water transportation worked well enough, both methods lacked the speed and convenience offered by a railway. Therefore, when the London & Birmingham Railway was opened in 1838, which passed through Leighton, great interest was shown by industrialists and local communities alike. One respected Luton gentleman, a Mr T. Austin, rode on horseback to Leighton and then travelled to London, via the new railroad, in order to witness the coronation of Queen Victoria.

In 1841 George and Robert Stephenson originated a scheme for a branch line from Leighton to Dunstable and Luton, which would give Luton a rail connection with London and Manchester. Their scheme gained the support of several influential Luton gentlemen, including Messrs Vyse, Ames, Thomson, Williamson and Austin.

A meeting was held at the George Hotel, Luton on 11th May, 1844 at which George Stephenson put forward his proposal. However, opposition to the plans developed, on the grounds that the line would have to intersect the Great Moor, a vast area of common land around the River Lea. The townsfolk had already relinquished the Little Moor for development and had allowed new roads to Bedford and Dunstable to cross the edge of the Great Moor. They were therefore unwilling to allow further breaking up of this space. At this opposition Stephenson, in an outburst of anger, warned the opponents of his scheme that Luton would not get its direct connection with London so long as he lived. This proved to be no idle threat, since when he died in 1848 Luton was still no nearer getting its direct rail link.

Dunstable was more fortunate, as on 30th June, 1845 the Royal Assent was given for the Dunstable, London & Birmingham Railway Act, with a capital of £50,000 which enabled the company to purchase the necessary land, build the line between Leighton and Dunstable and operate it when completed. This line terminated at street level beside the Watling Street in Dunstable and was opened on 1st June, 1848.

Meanwhile, a meeting had been held in Luton in 1845 to give consideration to the possibility of constructing a railway from Luton to Dunstable
which would link Luton with the London & Birmingham Railway, by way of
the Dunstable to Leighton branch line when it was built. The principal people attending this meeting were the Revd J. Little, the Revd H. Burgess and
Messrs Vyse, Waller, Williamson, Willis, How, Blundell, Brett, Bennett,
Jones, Jordan and Austin - most of whom were local businessmen.

This scheme also received opposition and a petition was raised by Mr
Charles Burr, in which he maintained that Luton needed a main line direct to
London and Manchester, and not a local branch line. Mr How supported the
petition and added 'that by connection with the London & Birmingham line
the journey from Luton to London would be 42 miles with one (if not two)
changes, whereas with the proposed direct line the journey would by only 28
miles'. He foresaw the awkward situation whereby Luton would be isolat-
ed, for 12 miles to the west was the London & Birmingham Railway, whilst
12 miles to the east the Great Northern Railway Company was building its
railway from London to York. (The first section from Peterborough to a temporary terminus at Maiden Lane, near Kings Cross, was opened on 7th
August 1850). Without a main line Mr How felt that local industrialists
would be compelled to move to one or other of these lines, thus discourag-
ing further development in Luton. After discussion the meeting adopted the
petition in favour of a direct line to London and Manchester.

Although Luton was left without its rail link other branch lines were being
built and company rivalry was rife. With a view to stopping any encroach-
ment by the London & North Western Railway Company (formerly the
London & Birmingham Railway Company) of the Great Northern Railway
Company's territory in the Home Counties, the Great Northern Railway
(Hertford, Hatfield and St Albans Branch) Act was placed on the Statute
Book on 22nd July, 1847. This authorised the building of a branch line from
St Albans to the Hertford station of the Hertford-Ware branch of the
Northern & Eastern Railway, with connections to the Great Northern in the
Hatfield district. However, progress was very slow - purchase of land still
being negotiated in 1853 - but eventually it was built and opened on 21st
October, 1865.

In the meantime, the compilers of the 1851 Census Return observed that
Luton was the largest town in the country without either railway or naviga-
ble water transport. There were some 16,000 inhabitants, turning out goods
to the value of £2,000,000 annually and it was becoming clear just how much
a railway link would benefit the town. The malt and flour producers of
North Hertfordshire were thinking along the same lines and in 1853 the people of Luton and Wheathampstead petitioned the Great Northern Railway
Company for a line to Hatfield, without success.

AN

ACT

For authorizing the Hertford, Luton, and Dunstable Railway Company to raise further Capital for the purposes of the Hertford Section of their Railway; and for Extending the Period for the Completion of the Luton Section of their Railway; and for other purposes.

𝖂𝖍𝖊𝖗𝖊𝖆𝖘 by the Hertford and Welwyn Junction Railway Act, 1854, the Hertford and Welwyn Junction Railway Company (since dissolved, and in this Act called the dissolved Hertford Company) were incorporated, and were authorized to make and maintain the Hertford 5 and Welwyn Junction Railway, and to raise a capital of Sixty-five Thousand Pounds by Three Thousand Two Hundred and Fifty shares of Twenty Pounds each, and to borrow not exceeding Twenty-one Thousand Six Hundred Pounds.

And Whereas the dissolved Hertford Company proceeded to 10 put that Act into execution, and they completed their line of railway and opened it for public use; but they incurred liabilities in respect thereto which are yet unsatisfied.

B

Front page of the Act authorising the Luton and Dunstable Railway to raise further capital.

However, when Parliamentary Notice was given indicating the intention of gaining powers to build a line from Hertford to Welwyn, the GNR wrote to the promoters in an effort to control their line, should it be built. The Hertford & Welwyn Junction Act of 3rd July, 1854 authorised the building of a line from the Northern & Eastern station at Hertford to a triangular junction at Digswell, on the Great Northern main line, with running powers into Digswell station.

During the first meeting of the Hertford & Welwyn Junction shareholders at Hertford on 30th September, 1854, those present were told that 'a line had recently been projected from Welwyn to Luton and Dunstable which would form an extension of the Hertford to Welwyn line, and have the effect of linking three great railways, i.e. the London & North Western at Dunstable, the Great Northern at Welwyn and the Eastern Counties at Hertford'. At this point the Great Northern Company made another offer - to work a Hatfield to Luton branch in the event of it being constructed, although they declined to back the venture financially.

The plans for the Dunstable line were deposited with the Clerks of the Peace in November 1854 and a company to administer the building of the line was formed at a meeting of the Hertford & Welwyn Junction Company on 25th June, 1855. The first Directors of this Company were the Hon. W. Cowper MP (Chairman), Mr Austin (Secretary) and Messrs Ames, Chambers, Lawes, Thomson and Waller - all of Luton.

The Act which authorised the construction of the Luton, Dunstable and Welwyn Junction Railway was passed on 16th July, 1855, and allowed for a connection with the London & North Western Railway at Dunstable and a triangular junction with the Great Northern Railway at Digswell, together with a bridge to carry the line over the Great Northern tracks to connect with the Hertford line. The Powers allowed for any of the three companies involved to work the line.

Naturally, the proposed railway aroused great interest and enthusiasm among the inhabitants of Luton, as the following Editorial from *The Luton Times* of July 1855 illustrates:

> Our railway has passed triumphantly through all its preliminary stages. The Royal Assent has been given and now the public have to deal with its interests in a fresh but not less inportant form. The question of pecuniary support as a matter of course stands on the threshold of the subject and we earnestly hope that many who are equally interested will now come forward and strengthen the hands of those who have been and still are earnestly striving to promote its success.
>
> As a stimulus to the tardy and a satisfaction to the suspicious, we are authorised to state that an offer has already been made by very responsible parties to lease the line for a good number of years at a rental of 5 per cent p.a.; this at once settles the question of a fair remuneration, and will, we trust, produce its legitimate result. Let

Luton, Dunstable & Welwyn Railway.

TURNING OF THE FIRST SOD,
25th October, 1855.

LADIES' TENT.

Admit the Bearer.

A 1910 postcard view of the Standbridge Road and Totternhoe Knolls, near Dunstable.
Authors' Collection

no man, we again intreat, be backward in making an effort, though at personal sac-
rifice for the time, to obtain a share in this important undertaking.

But considerations even more important than these present themselves, since
they have a bearing upon the future more than upon the present. Where shall we
have our station? is a question of immense interest in the town and neighbourhood
and we trust it will receive that amount of investigation and public attention which
so serious a matter requires. We understand a Public Meeting in to be held and public opinion invited, preparatory to which we would say - two places are mentioned:
7 Acres, at the top of Bute Street, and a meadow lately purchased by Mr Henry
Thomson of the Executors of the late Mr Lucas, Hitchin, and stretching nearly from
Dunstable Road on the one side to the New Road on the other side and bounded by
the Moor.

On behalf of the first site, it is advanced that its central position to the town and
neighbourhood recommends it. An objection to the latter is that its distance from
the centre of the town will render an Omnibus necessary, and an Omnibus fare is a
serious tax upon the community besides being a great inconvenience. We trust,
however, that the public themselves will take the matter up and by a seasonable
address to the Directors, prevent mistake on this intensely interesting and important
subject.

The Public Meeting referred to was held at short notice in Luton Town
Hall on Wednesday 10th October, 1855, and was 'numerously attended'. On
the platform were Mr E. Lucas (Chairman), Messrs R. How, W. Willis, F.
Brown, J. Everitt and W.H. Higgins. After much discussion only four people
voted for the amendment and the original motion was carried 'with accla-
mation'. Later, when shareholders met to consider the question of the station
site Messrs Thomson and Waller favoured the alternative site (opposite
Biscot Windmill), but where overwhelmingly defeated in the vote. They
resigned from the Board and their seats were taken by Messrs Sworder and
Everitt.

The contract for building the line was awarded to Messrs Jackson & Bean
and the Engineer was Mr John Cass Birkinshaw. The estimated cost of the
line (£120,000) provided for a single line and enough land to double it later.

The ceremony of cutting the first sod was performed in heavy rain by the
Rt Hon. William Cowper at the site of Hitchin Road Bridge on Thursday,
25th October 1855, and the people of Luton who had waited so long for their
railway went out of their way to celebrate the occasion. Shops closed at 1 pm
and the remainder of the day was observed as a public holiday. Despite the
poor weather (and the fact that, for all its enthusiasm, the local newspaper
had printed the wrong date in its announcement of the ceremony!) crowds
turned out to see a procession, headed by a Union Jack and banners pro-
claiming 'United We'll Succeed' and 'Hurrah for the Rail', followed by a
group of navvies carrying pickaxes and shovels and wearing new straw hats.
Dunstable Brass Band marched in the procession, which wound through the

streets to the Town Hall, where the Directors of the railway company joined in and made their way to the site.

At the site a 'commodious tent' had been erected for the ladies and a smaller one for the Directors and gentlemen connected with the company. Navvies gathered in an enclosure and a row of barrows, picks, shovels, planks, etc. indicated where the ceremony was to take place. At 3 o'clock, amidst the cheers of more than five thousand people, ringing church bells and a salute from a park of artillery stationed on Hart Hill, Cowper dug the first sod, placed it in a barrow and wheeled it to its destination. Other Directors followed and although their attempts at running the plank were not always successful they were greeted with good humoured shouts from the crowd. After addressing the assembled company from a barrow, Cowper rejoined the procession back to the Town Hall.

At 4 pm about 300 men gathered inside the Town Hall for a Dinner, the food being supplied by Mr Wadsworth of the George Hotel. The Rt Hon. William Cowper presided and Mr H. Brandreth was vice chairman. Tickets for this celebration were sold in advance at 3s. 6d. each, but this did not include wine.

The Luton company had notified land owners of its intention to purchase land for the section between Luton and Welwyn Junction but was unable to complete the deals once it had exhausted all its sources for borrowing money. It then tried to arrange a lease of the line with the London & North Western Railway Company - a proposal which was definitely turned down, but the company did offer to work the Dunstable to Luton line for two years.

The Luton and Hertford companies then commenced negotiations for an amalgamation of their two lines, a move which was bitterly opposed by Mr William Willis and a few of the Luton shareholders. The basis of their objection was the intention to provide a link between the Hertford & Welwyn line and the Eastern Counties Railway by way of a bridge over the Great Northern main line, thus forcing passengers to travel on the Eastern Counties line from Hertford to London instead of the Great Northern main line. However, other shareholders with the assistance of Messrs Jackson & Bean, who held about 4,000 shares in the Luton company, together with a considerable holding in the Hertford company, outvoted the opponents and the amalgamation Agreement was entered into. This voting took place at a meeting on 26th January, 1858 and many of the shareholders who opposed the proposals left the meeting without voting.

In spite of this vote, the bridge was not constructed, due to the conditions imposed by the Great Northern company; i.e. that it should be of one span only and should be built without interference to their main line trains. The approach embankment was built, however, in all probability with earth from Digswell cutting.

DUNSTABLE BRANCH RAILWAY,

TO THE

LONDON & BIRMINGHAM TRUNK, AT LEIGHTON-BUZZARD, BEDS.

CAPITAL, £60,000, IN 2,400 SHARES OF £25.
DEPOSIT, £1. 5s., PER SHARE.

PROVISIONAL COMMITTEE:

W. F. BROWN, Esq., *Dunstable.*
EDWARD BURR, Esq., *Dunstable.*
RICHARD GUTTERIDGE, Esq., *Dunstable.*
HENRY GOUDE, Esq., *Dunstable.*
JOHN COOPER, Esq., *Dunstable.*
JOHN PEARSE, Esq., *Dunstable.*
MR. WILLIAM ELLIOTT, *Dunstable.*

MR. JOHNSON MASTERS, *Dunstable.*
  „ EDWARD BEALE, *Luton.*
  „ BENJAMIN BENNETT, *Dunstable.*
  „ JOHN MELLOR, *Dunstable.*
  „ JOHN JOHNSON, *Dunstable.*
  „ GEORGE OSBORN, *Dunstable.*

ENGINEER:

GEORGE STEPHENSON, Esq.

SOLICITORS:

MR. JAMES N. CARTWRIGHT, *Dunstable.*
MESSRS. PARKER, HAYES, BARNWELL, and TWISDEN, 1, *Lincolns Inn Fields.*

BANKERS:

MESSRS. BASSETT, GRANT AND BASSETT, *Leighton-Buzzard and Dunstable.*

PARLIAMENTARY AGENTS:

MESSRS. BURKE, PRITT AND VENABLES, 44, *Parliament Street.*

(*Over.*

THIS RAILWAY is intended to join the LONDON AND BIRMINGHAM RAILWAY, at or near the Leighton-Buzzard Station, and to facilitate the communication from Dunstable and the Neighbourhood, with the more northern parts of England, and be the means of a speedy conveyance of the large and increasing manufacture of Straw Bonnets in the town of Dunstable and the Vicinity.

The importance of Dunstable as the first and best place of manufacture of the Dunstable Straw Plait, is well known and recognized throughout the Kingdom, and also as being the principal place for the manufacture of Whiting.

This line of Rail will also be the means of affording to the Town of Dunstable and the neighbourhood a much cheaper supply of Coals, Coke, Timber, Bricks, Slate, Lime, and all other goods and merchandise of heavy carriage; for all these various commodities there exists at present none but the most inefficient means of transit, it may therefore be fairly presumed, that upon the completion of a Railway, a great increase in the traffic of these articles will take place.

There is also in the immediate vicinity of Dunstable, and within 200 yards of the intended line, the Valuable Totternhoe Stone Quarries, which have supplied Stone for building most of the Churches and Mansions in the Neighbourhood.

A number of Shares are already taken—Application for Shares to be made to James N. CARTWRIGHT, Solicitor, Dunstable; or to Messrs. PARKER, HAYES, BARNWELL and TWISDEN, Solicitors, 1, Lincolns Inn Fields, London.

FORM OF APPLICATION.

TO THE PROVISIONAL COMMITTEE OF THE DUNSTABLE BRANCH RAILWAY,

I request that you will allot to me Shares in the Dunstable *Branch Railway, and I agree to take all such shares, (or so many thereof as you may allot to me,) and to pay the deposit, and sign the Parliamentary Contract, and Subscribers Agreement when required.*

Name
Residence
Trade or profession
Date

DUNSTABLE:—PRINTED BY T. PARTRIDGE, HIGH STREET.

The Prospectus for the Dunstable Branch Railway.

The Act confirming the amalgamation passed through Parliament on 28th June, 1858, with a capital of £185,000. The Hertford line had been opened to goods traffic on the last day of February 1858 and a passenger service started the following Monday. The Directors of the new company, called the Hertford & Luton & Dunstable Railway Company were the Rt Hon. W.F. Cowper, Thomas Chambers, Thomas Sworder, Lionel Ames and John Everitt. Lionel Ames became Chairman when Cowper resigned in September 1859.

The amalgamation allowed the company to raise more money to build the line from Luton to Welwyn Junction and they obtained permission to issue twelve thousand £10 shares. 8,816 were issued, but 1,816 were forfeited because the holders had not paid their dues, thus leaving 7,000 shares still valid. The residue were then offered to the existing shareholders, of which the Contractors took 4,000, bringing their holding in the company to just over three-quarters of the capital.

Meanwhile, work was in progress on the construction of the Luton to Dunstable section. During the excavations a male and a female skeleton, laying side by side, were found near Skimpot Farm (a 'find' which aroused considerable excitement in that area since a highwayman was reputed to have lived nearby).

Many men were employed in the building of the line but the hardest worked were obviously the navvies. A normal day's work for a pair of navvies involved filling 14 horse-drawn wagons with 20 tons of earth and rock, using only shovels, which had to be lifted above their heads during loading. Although the work was hard the pay was better than that of farm workers, ranging between 15s. (75p) and 22s. 6d. (£1.121/2) per week. Consequently many men left the farms to join a sub-contractor working on a local stretch of line, living practically without comforts in dirty wooden shanties, from which they broke out and drank to excess.

It is interesting to note that with the railway's arrival in Luton the local inhabitants became more police and crime conscious, which was understandable because the local constabulary was inexperienced and had only been formed in 1849. At its formation, Messrs Austin and Waller and several other local residents petitioned Quarter Sessions since they feared that Luton would get less protection than under the old system, when the township had one day constable and two night-watchmen. They urged, at least, that the Area Superintendent should have a means of speedy communication with his subordinates 'for which purpose they humbly suggest that he should be provided with a horse'. At this time the County Force totalled 47 men, of whom 41 were constables and six were Area Superintendents. Later, when the Midland Railway (Hitchin to Leicester, via Bedford) was being constructed Quarter Sessions agreed to enlist one extra constable!

With construction of the Luton to Dunstable section well under way an engine was employed to haul wagons from a ballast pit beside the Bedford Road. For many of the poorer people it was the first locomotive they had seen, and a crowd gathered to watch it working. At first they were frightened because 'to their astonishment it could go backwards as well as forwards'. However, when they saw how well the driver could control it they took a closer look - so close in fact that when it stopped to take water the area had to be boarded off to prevent accidents!

At the Half-Yearly Meeting of Shareholders, on 6th August, 1857, it was announced that the line between Luton and Dunstable was ready for goods traffic. In order that an inspection could be made several goods wagons were fitted with seats and about 40 shareholders took the opportunity to travel to Dunstable and back, the trip taking 12 1/2 minutes each way. On their return they expressed satisfaction with the efficient manner in which the work had been completed and commented on the smoothness of the journey.

Col Yolland inspected the line on 18th March, 1858 and his only adverse comments concerned small details, for example the lack of a clock at Luton. However, because the company intended to run engines tender-first on passenger trains he refused to pass the line for passenger usage until a turntable was built at Luton. On a visit a month later the Colonel passed the line, on an undertaking from officials of the Luton company that passenger trains would not be hauled by engines running tender-first. Turntables were later installed at both Luton and Dunstable.

A goods service was due to commence on 8th March, 1858 but owing to a dispute with the London & North Western Railway Company concerning the Dunstable terminus, and also a weak bridge, the start was delayed until 5th April, 1858.

After several announcements that the line was ready to take passengers and just as many announcements delaying the opening, a passenger service commenced on 3rd May,1858. To celebrate the opening, cheap tickets (3d. return) were made available and crowds of people flocked onto the station platforms. The first train ran from Luton and comprised two engines and 22 coaches, filled with excited passengers, many without tickets. The St Albans Brass Band travelled on the train to entertain the travellers, some of whom made the journey on the roof as there was no room available in the coaches.

The last train of that day was due to have left Dunstable for Luton at 9.30 pm but did not in fact leave until midnight. Although some people had walked home, those remaining were more than the train could accommodate and many were left behind.

Construction had commenced at the Welwyn end of the Luton line in April 1856 but by February 1858 little progress had been made, despite a report to

ANNO VICESIMO QUARTO

VICTORIÆ REGINÆ.

****

Cap. lxx.

An Act to vest in the *Great Northern* Railway Company the *Hertford, Luton, and Dunstable* Railway, and for other Purposes relating to the same Company   [12th *June* 1861.]

WHEREAS the Undertaking of the *Hertford, Luton, and Dunstable* Railway Company consists of Two Railways, the one (called the *Hertford and Welwyn Junction* Railway) connecting the *Great Northern* Railway at *Welwyn* in *Hertfordshire* with the *Eastern Counties* Railway at *Hertford*, the other (called the *Luton, Dunstable, and Welwyn Junction* Railway) connecting the *Great Northern* Railway, also at *Welwyn*, with the Undertaking of the *London and North-western* Railway Company at *Dunstable;* and the said Two Railways were amalgamated into One Undertaking in the Year One thousand eight hundred and fifty-eight, by the Name of the *Hertford, Luton, and Dunstable* Railway, but they were nevertheless for certain Purposes kept distinct, and separately designated as "The *Hertford* Section" and "The *Luton* Section," and their Capitals were also kept distinct, under the separate Designations of "*Hertford* Capital" and "*Luton* Capital:" And whereas it would conduce to the public Convenience, and to the efficient and economical Management of the said Railway, if it were transferred to the *Great Northern* Railway Company

17 & 18 Vict. c. cxxvii.

18 & 19 Vict. c. cxlvi.

21 & 22 Vict. c. lxxiv.

22 & 23 Vict. c. xxxiii.

[*Local.*]   10 *P*   upon

The Act to take over the local companies and absorb them into the GNR.

the shareholders that work would proceed. So little had in fact been done that the ceremony of cutting the sod was carried out for a second time on 28th January, 1859. In July the Powers to build the line expired and an application was made for an extension of time by two years. This extension was granted by an Act passed on 21st July,1859. By June 1860 the line was nearing completion and on 12th June a special train ran, enabling the London & North Western officials to inspect the new section, a special which aroused a great deal of public interest. Another special train ran on 17th July, carrying 160 Luton shareholders and calling at all stations along the line.

At a shareholders meeting in Luton on 24th February,1860 those present were told that the revenue from the Hertford line was £2,132, with expenses of £2,256 - resulting in a deficit of £124, whilst on the Luton line the income was £2,304 with expenses of £2,088 - leaving a balance of £216. Another meeting was held at the Great Northern Hotel on the 19th September to consider the £21,000 still owed by the company to the Contractors.

On 19th April, 1860 the Secretary of the Hertford & Luton & Dunstable Co. informed both the Eastern Counties Railway Company and the Great Northern Railway Company that the former was terminating the 1858 Agreement. On hearing this the Great Northern Company felt it was essential to take over the line, owing to its strategic importance between the Eastern Counties and London & North Western lines. A Bill was prepared to enable it to absorb the Hertford & Luton lines into the Great Northern network, although a clause was included which allowed them to withdraw the Bill should either of the former two Companies try to get running powers.

Just prior to opening the line the Great Northern Company found it necessary to build five gate-keepers' houses at various points along the line. Also, owing to the poor condition of the track, the Great Northern Company held the Hertford & Luton & Dunstable Company responsible for any accidents until it took over officially. In anticipation of opening, a Mr Bradley was appointed Agent for the Luton District at a salary of £180 per annum, plus £40 per annum house allowance and £20 travelling expenses.

The section between Luton and Welwyn Junction was opened for both goods and passenger use on 1st September,1860, under the name of the Hertford, Luton and Dunstable Railway, and at the same time Welwyn Junction station closed. Trains from Luton used the main line to go on to Hatfield, which arrangement continued until December 1868 when a separate line was opened for the branch, alongside the main line. The points connecting the branch to the main line were removed in January 1869. The first excursion over the new section of line ran to London on 18th September, with the cheapest fare 2s. 6d. (12 1/2p) and the dearest 3s. 6d. (17 1/2p).

It is said that some engineers referred to the line as the greatest feat of railway engineering work in England, because it was constructed at such a low cost per mile.

The arrangements for working the line by the Great Northern Railway Company were approved at a Shareholders' Meeting held in Luton on 22nd November, 1860. A Bill to this effect was given its second reading on 15th May, 1861 and became law when the Great Northern Railway Act was passed on 12th June, 1861. Although the Great Northern Company wanted exclusive powers over the line, a clause of the Act gave the London & North Western Company rights to send traffic between Luton and Dunstable.

With the new stretch of line open, Luton citizens again became anxious on the matter of police, or rather lack of police, and were continually pressing for an enlarged force to cope with the ever-growing population. They pointed out that 'since the opening of the railway from Luton to Hatfield, thieves have much greater facility in disposing of their plunder, by taking the early morning train to London before the police are aware of the transaction'. The County Force grew by degrees and in 1865 the Luton contingent numbered 15 men, but because in that year work was about to begin on the Midland Railway's line from Bedford to London (via Luton), in which work it was thought some 3,000 men would be employed, Quarter Sessions were again petitioned (this time by 40 Luton inhabitants) asking that their coverage be increased by five.

In order to understand the confusing situation which arose over the Dunstable stations it is better to go back in time and take a look at the problems as they happened. The London & North Western line from Leighton terminated in Dunstable beside the Watling Street and almost on the same level. It was therefore the original intention of the Welwyn Company to bring its line over the Watling Street to join directly onto the London & North Western line. This would have involved raising the road by 3 ft 8 in. and constructing a level crossing, but Parliament refused the application.

To overcome the problem, in 1856 Powers were obtained for a diversion of the line, crossing the Watling Street by a bridge, with the connection between the two lines taking place just west of the London & North Western Railway station. At this juncture, the LNWR requested that a new station be built by the Great Northern Company (which had in the meantime absorbed the Welwyn Company); Great Northern in turn offered to rebuild Church Street station as a joint venture. This proposal was accepted by the LNWR, provided it had equal rights within the station - a request to which the Great Northern Company would not accede, and hastily withdrew its offer. In spite of the inter-company squabble, Great Northern trains were still allowed to use the LNWR terminus, by reversing back into it, and eventually, after long and fruitless negotiations, the LNWR built a new station at Dunstable North, which was opened in January 1866.

As mentioned above, there was already a small station at Dunstable

Church Street, which opened in June 1858, but this was replaced by a new station just in time to appear in the timetables when the whole line opened. Presumably the Great Northern Company decided to 'go it alone' after negotiations with the London & North Western Company for a joint station failed. However, this new timber-built station soon proved unsuitable for its purpose and drew many complaints from passengers, and one wonders whether it really was an accident when it was burnt down in September 1871!

Accident or no accident, it certainly cleared the way for a more permanent station to be built. Rebuilding started in April 1872, when the weighbridge was moved to the other side of the yard and the booking office, a temporary wooden shed, was shifted bodily on rollers to make way for the foundations to be laid. The Contractors were Williams of Luton and the building cost £1,500.

Other building work was carried out at various points along the line in the early 1860s. Prior to 1863 only one platform existed at Luton station, but in that year a second platform was constructed on the up side of the line. The total cost of the station at Bute Street was £12,500. Harpenden and Wheathampstead were both served by temporary platforms until the Great Northern Company approved the construction of new ones. Tenders were sent out on Friday 23rd May, 1862, as a result of which the two stations were built, each costing £1,100.

During further building work at Harpenden (East) station in 1867 a pair of bronze bucket handles of Belgic workmanship were found. They have a design of rams' heads and are thought to have been the property of a wealthy farmer. Also found were parts of at least two wooden vessels, one evidently with an outer sheath of bronze, and a hinge-like object which was probably fixed to the lip of a ceremonial bowl. A little further north at Coldharbour (Harpenden) a Roman lamp was discovered in the railway embankment.

By April 1868 construction of the Midland main line from Bedford to London was sufficiently advanced to allow the opening of a footbridge linking Bute Street to High Town Road in Luton and giving access to the Midland and Great Northern stations. This bridge was later rebuilt and the new one opened on Wednesday 8th August, 1877.

Before the Midland line came to Luton its traffic had run from Bedford to Hitchin and then on to London via the Great Northern line, but the Great Northern Company blatantly gave priority to its own trains. This was one of the principal reasons for the Midland Company deciding to build its own line to London, a decision which created problems for the Great Northern Company at Luton, since the Midland route was more direct.

Despite the intrusion of the Midland Railway, traffic was increasing on the Great Northern main line towards the end of the 19th century, to an extent

An 1887 view of the 'Cock Pond', Harpenden.   *Authors' Collection*

The River Lea at Harpenden, with the railway and goods shed in the background, *c.*
1910.   *Authors' Collection*

that it was necessary to provide additional lines. In order to achieve this the formation between Hatfield and Digswell had to be widened so that a new track could be constructed for the Dunstable branch - the old Dunstable line becoming the new down slow line. The Agreement for this work was dated 18th February, 1895 and showed that the builders were Henry Osbourne Baldry and John Eardley Yerburgh, both of 21 Queen Anne's Gate, Westminster (Messrs Baldry & Yerburgh, general contractors), and the distance involved was two miles and fifty-one chains.

For the sum of £17,383 they were to construct the embankment, bridges and fences, and provide all the necessary plant, materials and labour. It was agreed in the Specification that the line would be completed to the satisfaction of the Engineer and would be handed over to the company fit for passenger traffic on or before 30th November, 1895, the Contractors maintaining all works for 12 calendar months thereafter.

The Specification, dated the 2nd January 1895, referred to the construction and maintenance of 'A line of railway with bridges, cuttings and embankments, and all works connected therewith' but the Contractors were not required to supply 'permanent way materials and fastenings and ballast'. This meant that the Contractors would undertake the structural work and Great Northern employees would construct the actual railway.

The following are extracts from the Specification:

> Formation, metalling and maintaining as long as may be requisite of all temporary bridges and roads and of all temporary or permanent diversions and alterations of roads, pathways, gutters or watercourses and the reinstating of the same in their original position before the completion of the Contract.
>
> The excavations and earthwork for all foundations, the laying of drainpipes, the foundations of walls, piers, abutments and other similar works throughout the whole extent of the Contract together with the removal of all surplus materials. The construction of all roadways, paths, culverts, and sewers, all works necessary for shoring and under-pinning and erection of retaining walls and the providing and laying in of all drainpipes that may be required or ordered. All signals will be provided and fixed by the Company (GNR), all the permanent way including top ballast, the laying in of switches, crossings etc. will be provided and done by the Company. The Contractor to accommodate all workmen, navvies and labourers of every class at a moderate rent and no huts or hovels will on any account be permitted on any part of the line.'
>
> Engineer may inspect accommodation and order the Contractor to arrange medical attendance and the Engineer to be informed of these arrangements. Workmen to be paid in full in money at least once a fortnight and not by provisions, liquor or goods. To be paid in an office built for the purpose of paying the men and not in a public house or other place where intoxicating liquor may be sold.
>
> Contractor liable for safety of existing line.
>
> Tender must be made upon the provided form accompanying this Specification from which it must not be detached. It must be enclosed, sealed up, endorsed 'GNR

Tender for widening at Hatfield' and delivered to the Secretary's Office, Kings Cross Station, London before Ten am on the 3rd January, 1895 and parties tendering must be in attendance at that time. The Directors do not bind themselves to accept the lowest or any Tender.

No passes for Contractor, workmen or materials will be issued by the Company. All materials for the works must be consigned to Hatfield, the Contractor must lay in proper sidings where required and most convenient to the Company. All old material to remain the property of the Company.

Schedule of Company's Charges

Hire of Company's Locomotive	10s.	
Hire of 5-ton Travelling Hand Crane................(per day).........	10s.	6d.
Hire of 15-ton Travelling Steam Crane..............(per day)......... £2.	10s.	
Wages of Foremen ....(per day).........	5s.	
Wages of Guard or Brakesmen...........................(per day).........	5s.	
Ashes...(per ton)	2s.	6d.

Sunday - Time and a half
1 Day equals 10 hours
Time of loco hire reckoned from departure until return to engine shed

Widening at Hatfield

SUMMARY OF BILLS OF QUANTITIES
B.S. Brundell, Surveyor, Doncaster

	£	s.	d.
Extracts from Specification	256	6	6
Earthworks	3,145	12	6
Forming and Burnt Ballasting	2,163	16	0
Fencing and Ditching	1,039	15	2
Drainage	1,768	3	3
Bridge at 18 miles 2 chains	732	6	6
Bridge at 18 miles 40 chains	833	3	1
Bridge at 18 miles 58 chains	3,619	11	7
Bridge at 18 miles 74 chains	854	7	7
Bridge at 19 miles 37 chains	586	15	2
Bridge at 19 miles 65 chains	336	19	4
Maintenance	75	0	0
Daywork Charges	616	13	4
Materials on ground	1,354	10	0
Total	**17,383**	**0**	**0**

SCHEDULE OF DAYWORK COSTS

Hours		Per Hour	£	s.	d.
1,000	Navvies	6d.	25	0	0
1,000	Labourers	6d.	25	0	0
1,000	Blacksmiths	9d.	37	10	0
1,000	Strikers	6d.	25	0	0
1,000	Plumbers	8d.	33	6	8
1,000	Bricklayers	10d.	41	13	4
1,000	Masons	9d.	37	10	0
1,000	Slaters	8d.	33	6	8
1,000	Joiners	9d.	37	10	0
1,000	Carpenters	9d.	37	10	0
1,000	Painters	6d.	25	0	0
1,000	Watchmen	4d.	16	13	4
1,000	Boys	3d.	12	10	0
1,000	Rivetters	9d.	37	10	0
1,000	Holders-Up	6d.	25	0	0
1,000	Rivet-Boys	3d.	12	10	0
1,000	Platers	7d.	29	3	4

Days					
100	One-Horse cart & Driver, per day of 10 hrs. at 10s.		50	0	0
100	Two-Horse cart & driver, per day of 10 hrs. at 15s.		75	0	0
		Total	616	13	4

MATERIALS ON GROUND

			£	s.	d.
20,000	Stock Bricks	@ 30s. per 1,000	30	0	0
20,000	Blue Staffs Bricks	@ 60s. per 1,000	60	0	0
10,000	Pressed Blue Staffs Bricks	@ 75s. per 1,000	37	10	0
1,000	Plinth Bricks	@ 90s. per 1,000	4	10	0
1,000	Coping Bricks	@ 100s. per 1,000	5	0	0
100 tons	Portland Cement	@ 35s. per ton	175	0	0
500 cu. yds.	Thames Ballast	@ 4s. per cu. yd	100	0	0
500 cu. yds.	Gravel Ballast	@ 4s. per cu. yd	100	0	0
5,000 cu. yds.	Burnt Ballast	@ 2s. 6d. per cu. yd	625	0	0
1,000 cu. yds.	Sand	@ 1s. per cu. yd	50	0	0
100 linear yds.	12" pipe	@ 3s. per lin. yd	15	0	0
100 linear yds.	9" pipe	@ 2s. per lin. yd	10	0	0
100 linear yds.	18" pipe	@ 4s. 6d. per lin. yd	22	10	0
100 linear yds.	6" pipe	@ 1s. 6d. per lin. yd	7	10	0
100 linear yds	4" pipe	@ 1s. per lin. yd	5	0	0
100	12" to 6":junctions	@ 4s. each	20	0	0
100	12" to 4" junctions	@ 4s. each	20	0	0
100	12" bends	@ 3s. each	15	0	0
100 linear yds.	9" half-round pipes	@ 2s. 6d. per lin. yd	12	10	0
200 cu. ft	copings etc.	@ 4s. per cu. ft	40	0	0
		Total	1,354	10	0

The question of doubling the whole line from Hatfield to Dunstable was raised many times. In 1890 between 400 and 500 season ticket holders used the Luton to Dunstable section and this was considered sufficient justification for doubling that length of line. However, the only progress made in that direction came about a little later when, in 1891, Powers were obtained for purchasing land to allow a second track to be constructed from Luton Station as far as Brown & Sons' Timber Siding, a distance of about half a mile. In 1895 and 1898 extensions of time were granted and eventually the work started during May 1898.

The Contract was awarded to Mr Mousley, of Huntingdon, and the Resident Engineer was Mr Cross. During November 1898 a new girder bridge was installed over Dunstable Road and the old bridge removed, giving a much better alignment to the road and wider pavements (by all accounts, not before time!). Guildford Street bridge was also widened to take five tracks - the double line and three sidings - making it the widest bridge in the town, and a new signal box was built at Luton West. The double line which cost approximately £100,000 to build was opened at noon on 10th September, 1899.

Whilst the work was in progress a deputation from Dunstable Town Council called on the Directors of the Great Northern Railway Company, on 17th March, 1899, to ask them to double the line as far as Hatfield, but although they were received courteously their proposition received little sympathy. However, the Directors did agree to print some posters of Dunstable and surrounding beauty spots in an endeavour to publicise Dunstable as a holiday town!

It would appear that the question of a double line was often discussed, but perhaps the Mayor of Luton summed it up when addressing a Great Northern Railway Dinner in 1914. Advocating the doubling of the line throughout, he added 'but it is such a profitable line that the Company dare not disturb it'.

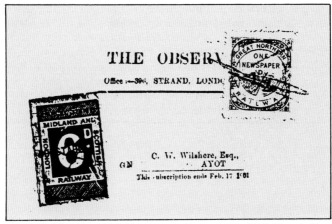

Newspaper Label bearing GN Newspaper Stamp with LMS Parcel Stamp (ex-Dunstable) superimposed.

Chapter Two

Route

A Route Plan and Station Diagrams are included, which should be studied in conjunction with the following description of the route of the two branch lines. In order to simplify this description in relation to the plans, let us start at the old market town of Hatfield and work along the line. Here stood the engine sheds which had been built to house the engines which worked the three branch lines radiating from Hatfield: to Hertford, St Albans and Dunstable. Both St Albans and Dunstable branch line trains used the west side of the down main platform (known as the Western Platform) at the main line station, and originally trains from London, bound for the branches, were unable to make a direct connection therewith. The next track over from the platform was the down goods line, but from the 28th November, 1937 this was made into the down slow line from Redhall to Hatfield, and in 1941 a connection was put in between this and the Western Platform line, simplifying through working.

The St Albans line branched off just north of Hatfield station, but the Dunstable line continued on under Wrestlers Bridge and ran parallel to the main line to Welwyn Garden City, where the branch was served by the rear half of the main line station's down slow platform. From here the line turned sharply westwards by the 20½ milepost, passing four platelayers' cottages, to a level crossing. Known as Lyle's Crossing, it was provided with a keeper's hut, but the need for this ceased when Digswell Road and the new White Bridge were built - opened by Sir Henry Maybury in November 1925. When Queen Elizabeth II visited Welwyn Garden City to open the new hospital, on 22nd July, 1963, her car was halted on this bridge so that she could admire the view down Parkway to the fountain which had been installed to commemorate her Coronation.

Returning to the branch, the line climbed steeply through Brocks Wood, a very picturesque area, with many fine fir and silver birch trees, and primroses in spring. In these woods were three swallow-holes, one of which was directly beside the line, and must have created problems when it came to erecting the railway fence, for at times it contained as much as 20 ft of water. A short way up the incline was a farm siding, relaid and extended in 1920 to serve a builder's yard, and latterly used as a coal yard.

Almost at the top of the incline, which started at 1 in 56 and eased to 1 in 162, the line ran under the Great North Road (A1), and into Ayot station, which until April 1878 was known as Ayott St Peter. In the early days of the line the station buildings occupied only one platform, on the down side, but in 1892 a passing loop was installed and a platform constructed on the up

Class 'A4', No. 60021 *Wild Swan* on an up express passing Hatfield on 11th September, 1961. The Luton platform is on the left of the island platform. *Oakwood Collection*

Class 'N2' 0-6-2T No. 69534 on the 6.07 pm passenger service from Hatfield to Dunstable, at Welwyn Garden City on 9th June, 1951. *Lens of Sutton*

A view in 1919 of the site of the 'first' Welwyn Garden City station and the junction. The Luton line branches to the left, whilst the Hertford branch is seen to the right.

Authors' Collection

Welwyn Garden City showing the Luton branch curving off westwards. *Reproduced from the 25 in., 1923 Ordnance Survey map*

A further view of the GNR main line *c*. 1919, at Welwyn Garden City, looking north. The first station platform appears in the middle of the photograph and the Luton branch curves away to the left. The Luton platform for Welwyn Garden City station (*seen below*) was built on the curve of the branch.   *Top: D. White, bottom: E. Miller*

Just rounding the curve of the Luton branch, a local service is approaching Welwyn Garden City station in 1926. Obviously a well patronised service in those days!

D. White

A 1921 view, looking across the GNR main line, of the branch station at Welwyn Garden City. *K.A. Ladbury*

A fine view taken in 1910 of Ayot station, looking west.   *D. White*

An up passenger service passing Ayot signal box on 20th June, 1960.

J. Spencer Gilkes

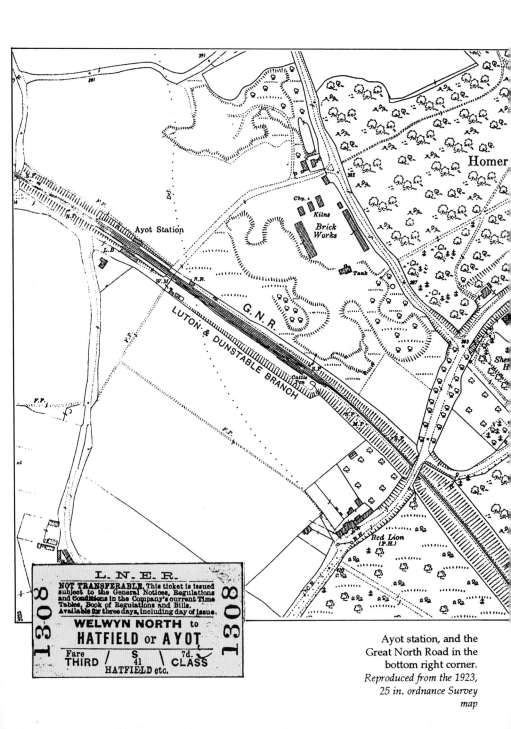

Homer

Ayot Station

Chy.

Kilns

Brick
Works

Tank

G.N.R.

LUTON & DUNSTABLE BRANCH

Cattle
Pen

Red Lion
(P.H.)

L.B.

W.M.

S.B.

F.P.

F.P.

391

391

L. N. E. R.

NOT TRANSFERABLE This ticket is issued
subject to the General Notices, Regulations
and Conditions in the Company's current Time
Tables, Book of Regulations and Bills.
Available for three days, including day of issue.

WELWYN NORTH to
HATFIELD or AYOT

Fare   S   7d.
THIRD   /   41   \   CLASS
        HATFIELD etc.

1308

1308

Ayot station, and the
Great North Road in the
bottom right corner.
*Reproduced from the 1923,
25 in. ordnance Survey
map*

The entrance to the siding into Blackbridge Dump. The Luton branch is on the left. *Authors*

Blackbridge Dump as seen in February, 1970. *Authors*

Marford crossing gate keeper's house, 29th January, 1967. *Authors*

A view of the station house and station buildings (*right*) at Wheathampstead in 1950.
Authors' Collection

Class 'N7' 0-6-2T No. 69695 stands at Wheathampstead station with the 1.40 pm service for Dunstable on 6th May, 1960. *Paul Waldock*

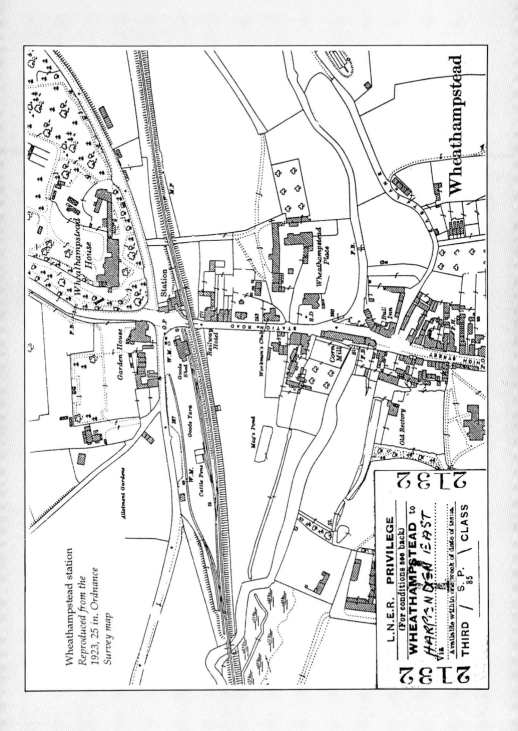

Wheathampstead station
Reproduced from the
1923, 25 in. Ordnance
Survey map

Wheathampstead

Wheathampstead House

Garden House

Allotment Gardens

Goods Shed

Goods Yard

Cattle Pens

Station

Railway Hotel

Map's Pond

Wheathampstead Place

Workman's Club

Corn Mill

Old Rectory

Bull Inn

STATION ROAD

2132

L.N.E.R. PRIVILEGE
(For conditions see back)
WHEATHAMPSTEAD to
HARPENDEN EAST
Via
Available within one week of date of issue.
THIRD / S.P. \ CLASS
85

2132

Running bunker first, the Hatfield train coasts into Wheathampstead station in 1948. Note the changing gradient! *A. Willmott*

An official GNR postcard of 1905 portraying a down train entering Wheathampstead station. *Authors' Collection*

Wheathampstead. Station, G. N. R.

Viewed from the train as it approaches Wheathampstead station, this view shows the
road bridge and station buildings. *A. Willmott*

A final view of Wheathampstead station in GNR days. *Authors' Collection*

799   WHEATHAMPSTEAD STATION.

A locally produced postcard of Harpenden station, with a down train approaching, *c.* 1930.   *Authors' Collection*

A view of Harpenden East station, looking towards Luton in 1963. Note the goods shed on the right.   *Les Casey*

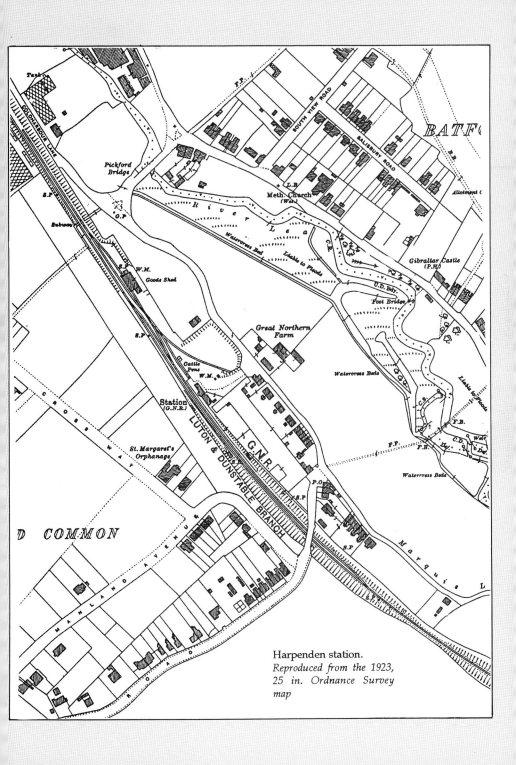

Harpenden station.
*Reproduced from the 1923,
25 in. Ordnance Survey
map*

GER horsebox special train from Newmarket at Harpenden on 27th May, 1907.
Authors' Collection

The 2.21 pm Dunstable to Hatfield crosses the pick-up goods at Harpenden on 25th June, 1960. *Authors' Collection*

side, together with a new signal box. These structures remained until they were destroyed by fire on 26th July, 1948. The following report is taken from a local newspaper:

> The 'wooden box' railway station at Ayot was gutted by fire on Monday morning. During the two-hour blaze smoke and flame enveloped the station and the smell of burning creosote drifted for miles. Firemen struggled across fields with hydrants but the all-wooden structure defeated them; only cinders and a chimney stack remained of the up platform with its waiting room. Spectators helped the firemen handle a pump and hoses over the burning track and across the fields to a nearby pond. The down platform, waiting room and booking office were severely damaged. Flames spread along the sleepers and the track curled and buckled in the heat. An emergency gang from Hitchin found the lines three feet out of true. They restored service during the afternoon. Firemen from Welwyn Garden City, Hatfield, Welwyn, Stevenage, Harpenden and St Albans were there. The Welwyn brigade was the first there. A porter spotted the fire at 10.33 am, just after a passenger train had left. With signalman, George Hercock, he fought with extinguishers but when the fire got out of hand they called the brigades and began to salvage stores.

It appears that news of the fire travelled almost as quickly as the fire itself - only 12 minutes after the fire was discovered Mrs Lantin, who lived at the Station House, received a telephone call from her husband (a clerk at Liverpool Street station) asking if the house was safe!

In fact, the house was unharmed but all that remained of the station were the brick-built toilets on the down platform and the concrete block foundations, which were still evident many years later. The station was not rebuilt and subsequently closed to passenger traffic on 26th September, 1949.

On leaving Ayot, the line passed round the back of Ayot St Peter, by the site of Robinsons Wood Siding, to Blackbridge Sidings. Here a wide footbridge spanned the line at the point of the first sidings - these sidings being provided with a run-round loop. The second siding was situated by Marford Crossing gatekeeper's house, but was removed when this part of the gravel quarry became exhausted.

Wheathampstead station stood on the up side of the line, just south of Station Road bridge, and access was gained via three flights of wooden steps. Originally, the ticket office was at the foot of the steps but in 1881 it was incorporated into the station buildings at platform level. The principal station buildings were of timber construction and the roof partially covered the platform. The platform itself was of solid construction, being brick-based with square stone capping. This capping was later replaced by ornate stonework and overhanging concrete slabs. Fencing consisted of concrete posts and iron tube railings, on which the station lights were affixed. There were two large nameplates and some smaller ones attached to lamp-posts.

The station was backed by fir trees, concealing the station master's house, which stood at the corner of Codicote Road and Station Road.

The goods yard, to the west of Station Road bridge, consisted of three long sidings; the one furthest from the branch line being the coal siding. Another siding ran into the goods shed and also served the unloading dock. A short siding ran up to this dock, known locally as 'the Dung Road' because this was where manure wagons were unloaded. The unloading dock was partially covered, with the remainder taken up by cattle pens.

Stables for shunting horses were situated behind the coal siding, close to the Lower Luton Road. A weighbridge which stood near the stable was taken out about 1930, but the weighbridge near the main entrance to the goods yard remained in use - its hut being used as an office by the local coal merchant. Originally trains could gain access to the yard at two places but the south end points were removed in 1963.

On leaving Wheathampstead the line crossed the River Lea by means of a two-arch brick and girder bridge. Just beyond this the line was crossed by a footpath to Wheathampstead village, guarded by a wide gate and kiss-gates on either side, set at an angle to the line. This path was often used by children and their safety became the concern of the Parish Church authorities. So much pressure was brought to bear on the railway company that a tiny subway, only six feet wide and six feet high, was excavated. In the south wall of the subway was a small cavity which housed an oil lamp and kiss-gates were put at both entrances. As the subway was below the level of the river a raised cast iron floor was put in to allow flood water to lay underneath. This water was then pumped out by means of a hand-pump. The task of pumping and lamp tending was carried out by a porter from Wheathampstead.

Continuing in a north-westerly direction, for the most part alongside the River Lea, the line passed over Leasey Bridge level crossing, beside which stood a gatekeeper's cottage and hut.

Harpenden East, the next station, was built in a shallow cutting and provided a passing loop. The station buildings were situated on the up side of the line, whilst the signal box stood at the south end of the down platform. The platforms, again solid, were simple brick walls with stone slab capping and a tarmacadam surface. There was one large nameplate on the down platform, another affixed to the station buildings and small nameplates attached to the lamp-posts. Electric lights replaced the oil lamps in 1937.

The goods yard, to the north of the up platform, consisted of a loop, with a headshunt beyond, and two short sidings. The rear siding was used for coal, the other served the cattle dock. Straddling one side of the loop was the goods shed, with an unloading crane inside. A hut adjoining the goods shed was originally used for stabling shunting horses but in latter days was used by platelayers. For many years an old goods van body stood at the back of the yard, housing firewood and straw. At the station entrance was a weigh-bridge with a hut beside it and a large sleeper-built coal bunker behind it.

In 1894 a subway was constructed, just north of the station, for the use of farmers herding their cattle and sheep between Batford and Manland Common. Later three kiss-gates were erected - one on each boundary and one on the west entrance to the subway.

At the Hertfordshire/Bedfordshire border a short siding served Coles' Mill. Permission for this was obtained from Sir John Leigh of Luton Hoo. It came into use on 22nd June, 1865 and was removed in 1962.

Some two miles from Harpenden the branch was crossed by the Midland main line. The next station, Luton Hoo, formerly New Mill End, was built on the down side of the line and the platform was identical to that at Wheathampstead. Half the platform was covered by a roof which extended back to give a covered entrance-way. The ticket office, waiting room and toi-lets were situated under the roofed section, with the station master's house and outbuildings extending along the remainder of the platform. At the north end of the station was a level crossing, with the goods yard beyond. This yard consisted of two sidings, one with a cattle dock and a headshunt. An old wagon body, used as a shed, stood in the yard with a prefabricated platelayers' hut beside it.

Continuing towards Luton, the line once more crossed the River Lea and the B653 road, passed through tall beech trees bordering the Luton Hoo Estate and from this point followed the bank of the Midland main line to Vauxhall Motors' sidings. Just south of Luton Bute Street station was the Great Northern Railway coalyard.

Luton Bute Street station was approached from a large forecourt, which also served the loading dock and a siding. A footbridge from the forecourt crossed the line, the road and the Midland main line, to High Town, and pro-vided access to the three Great Northern platforms. Very close to the foot-bridge steps on No. 1 Platform was a water column. Also on this platform were the station buildings, consisting of a waiting room, booking office, parcels room and refreshment room, the latter being opened in December 1886. The up line was served by an island platform, the back of which served a siding. A waiting room and railway police offices were later built on this 'island'. All three platforms were covered; the roof of platform 1 being a canopy and that of platforms 2 and 3 being supported on central posts. The platforms were surfaced with large concrete slabs.

Bute Street station was repainted in September 1876 and in the words of a local newspaper 'those who know the station will not need to be told that the improvement is not being effected before it was required'!

Immediately north of the station was a large brick building bearing the

GNR No. 1247 approaching Luton Hoo on the special service in April 1962.
Authors' Collection

The station buildings at Luton Hoo as seen from the station yard.   *Authors' Collection*

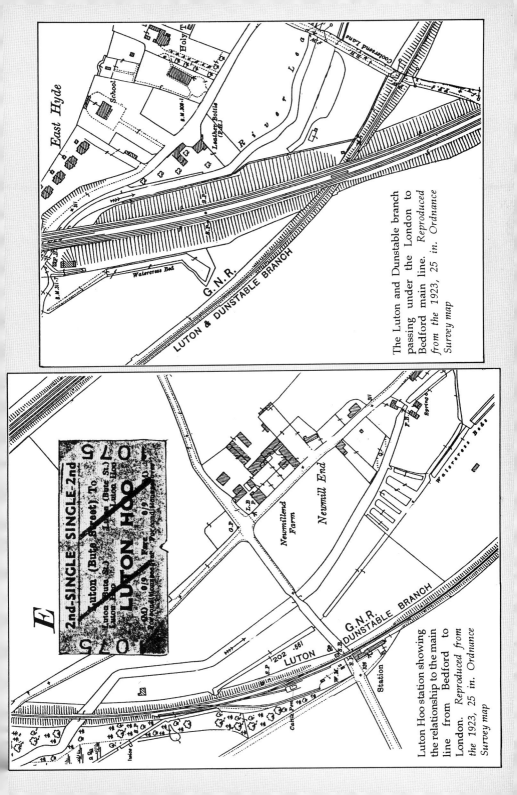

East Hyde

The Luton and Dunstable branch passing under the London to Bedford main line. Reproduced from the 1923, 25 in. Ordnance Survey map

Luton Hoo station showing the relationship to the main line from Bedford to London. Reproduced from the 1923, 25 in. Ordnance Survey map

Hayward and Tyler's Factory, Luton 1907.   *T. Hobbs*

An up local service passing Vauxhall sidings, Luton.   *Authors' Collection*

Tank Wagons for Laportes seen here at Luton Bute Street, 14th April, 1962.   *K. Taylor*

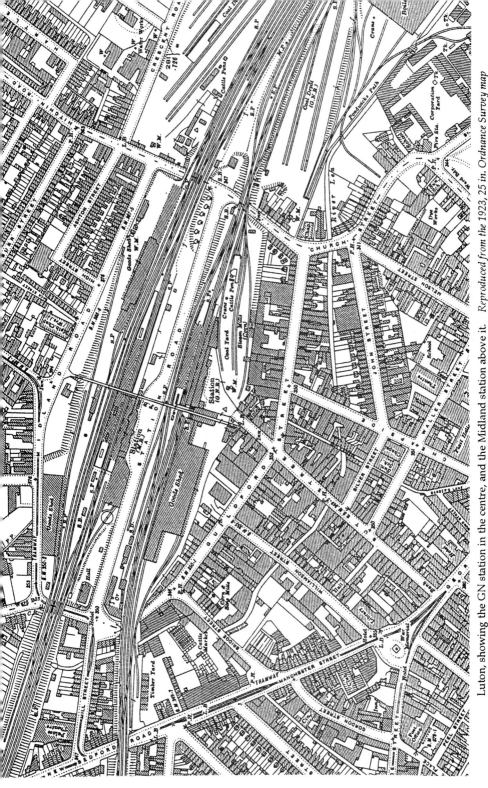

Luton, showing the GN station in the centre, and the Midland station above it. *Reproduced from the 1923, 25 in. Ordnance Survey map*

Luton Bute Street, looking towards Luton Yard signal box in the 1950s. *Lens of Sutton*

Another view of Luton Bute Street, this time from the footbridge in 1966. *K. Taylor*

Fireless locomotive GFN 3 seen here at Laportes Sidings, Luton. This locomotive was
built by Andrew Barclay, Works No. 1477/16.   *R. Flanagan*

A football special from
Wolverhampton, crossing
the 'new' M1 road bridge
in 1960. *Authors' Collection*

Class 'N7' 0-6-2T No. 69639 passing Chaul End signal box on 29th September, 1956.
S. Summerson

Two views of Dunstable Town station in January, 1967. (*Above*) looking westwards and (*below*) looking east.   *H. Ramsey*

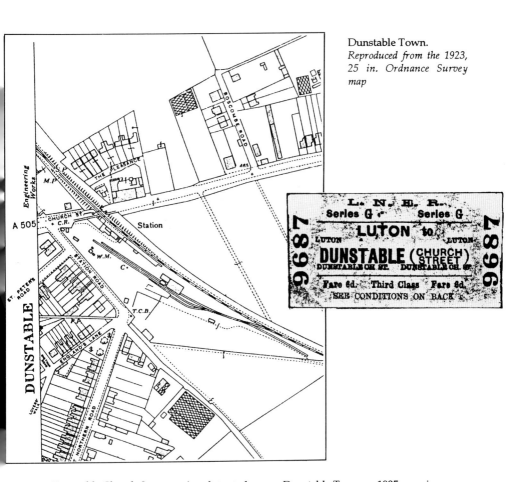

Dunstable Town.
Reproduced from the 1923, 25 in. Ordnance Survey map

Dunstable Church Street station, later to become Dunstable Town, *c.* 1905 seen in an old postcard.   *Authors' Collection*

DUNSTABLE TOWN

A GNR crane sits in the goods yard at Dunstable Town station on 18th January, 1967.
H. Ramsey

Vauxhall Sidings ground frame at Dunstable seen here in 1978.   *Authors*

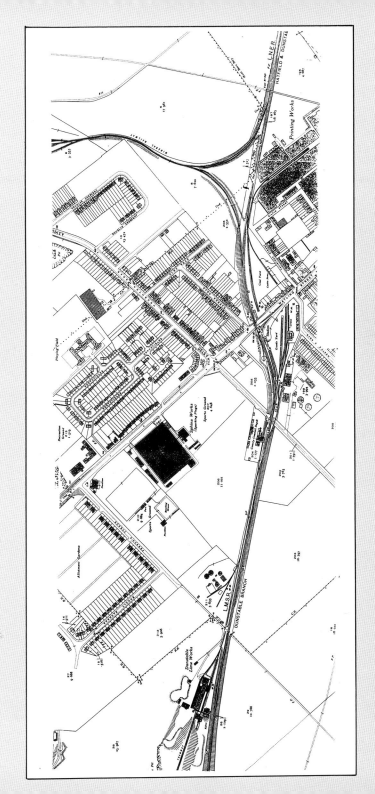

Dunstable (North) station in the middle and, to the east, the triangle and siding to the Cement Works. To the west are the quarry and works of the Dunstable Lime Works at the top of Sewell Bank. *Reproduced from the 1928, 25 in. Ordnance Survey map*

Train leaving Dunstable North for Leighton Buzzard in 1950.   *P. Gomm*

A general view of Dunstable North station from the old signal box in 1957.   *B. Parnell*

A dmu special train approaching Dunstable North station on 19th October, 1968.

H. Ramsey

No. 69588, 0-6-2T class 'N1' from Hatfield (*left*) and the Leighton Buzzard service standing (*right*) in 1952 at Dunstable North station.   *G. Goslin*

A Leighton Buzzard local service descending Sewell Bank near Dunstable, 1960.

P. Gomm

The diminutive station buildings at Stanbridgeford seen on 26th May, 1956.

H.C. Casserley

words 'London & North Eastern Goods and Bonded Warehouse', these
words remaining long after nationalisation. From Bute Street the line continued through Luton passing the Football Ground and Laporte's chemical
works, to Chaul End level crossing. Here, on the up side of the line, stood a
signal box with a gatekeeper's house opposite. About three-quarters of a
mile further on a new bridge was constructed to carry the line over the M1
Motorway.

At Skimpot two sidings served a warehouse, which was opened as a
refrigeration depot for meat in 1941. In 1966 the London Railway
Preservation Society stored their locomotives and coaches at these sidings,
but during the last week of April 1969 all their stock was removed by road
and delivered to their new base at Quainton Road, Aylesbury. On the down
side of the line, at the foot of Blows Down, a long siding served a chalk quarry on land owned by Skimpot Farm. (On the 1894 map the area is named
Skimpool Farm.)

The branch wound its way on round the foothills of Dunstable Downs to
Dunstable Town station, which comprised a single platform of timber construction sited on the down side, immediately above the Luton-Dunstable
road. Two sidings ran down the centre of the yard behind the station and
one served the goods shed. A small crane stood in the yard near the station
buildings, to which a new jib was fitted in September 1914.

Before reaching Dunstable North station the line passed Vauxhall Motors'
Dunstable Works and sidings which served Houghton Regis Cement Works.
It then crossed the A5, Watling Street, by a bridge and ran straight into
Dunstable North station, where Hatfield trains terminated and connected
with trains for Leighton (Buzzard). On the down side were two platforms
and a bay. Hatfield trains used the down platform and Leighton trains used
the bay. It is believed the up platform was never used by passengers,
although the track was used as a run-round loop, at the end of which was a
small turntable. The Great Northern goods yard was sited just before the
Watling Street bridge and the London & North Western goods yard and coal
sidings were behind the station. A level crossing just beyond the station was
controlled from Dunstable North signal box.

The section from Dunstable to Leighton Buzzard was double-track
throughout, and encountered several steep gradients. The line left Dunstable
on a slight incline for a short distance and then ran down a 1 in 40 gradient
for about a mile, past Totternhoe Chalk Quarries, to level ground near
Gowers' Siding. A small signal box on the down side controlled access to the
exchange sidings from the quarries.

A short distance further on was Stanbridgeford station, with its level crossing and small goods yard. The station house was adjacent to the crossing on
the down side and the two platforms were laid with small square stone

blocks. The next level crossing and gatekeeper's house were at Stanbridge
Mead, where the gates were against road traffic for most of the time, as staff
received no warning of oncoming trains. Beyond this, at Billington Road
level crossing, on the outskirts of Leighton Buzzard, there was also a gatekeeper's house, a small lever frame and a shed.

The line then ran between several large sand pits, with sidings leading off
in several directions. One of these was served by an extensive narrow gauge
railway system. These sidings provided a great deal of traffic for the four
sidings of Grovebury Crossing goods yard. Beyond the level crossing at
Grovebury Road the line kept straight and ran up a 1 in 220 incline to the
double arched bridge over the River Ouzel and Grand Union Canal. Just
before the bridge a short siding ran alongside the narrow gauge line from
Rackley Hill Pits for exchange purposes.

Once over the bridge, the line descended, again at 1 in 220, to Ledburn
Crossing, where the coal yard was served by two short sidings. These ran
back as far as the old London & North Western pumping station situated
halfway down the gradient. The wells were on the opposite side of the line.
Although the pipes and valves remained when the line closed, the buildings
were demolished long before and the wells filled in. From Ledburn Crossing
the branch crossed the A418 at Wing Crossing, rounded a sharp bend on a 1
in 80 gradient and ran into Leighton Buzzard station.

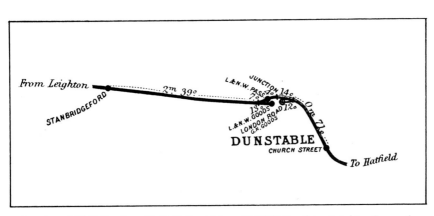

Junction of GNR line from Hatfield (*to right*) and LNWR line from Leighton Buzzard
(*left*), reproduced from a 1903 RCH map.

Chapter Three

Signalling

At the beginning the two railway companies were responsible for signalling their own lengths of line, but it seems that as time went by and signals were replaced for one reason or another no set pattern or style emerged. In fact a great variety of signals appeared, some of which are described in detail in this chapter.

When the Hatfield to Luton section was built Great Northern slotted signals were used but these were hastily withdrawn following the Abbots Ripton crash of 1876, and in their place came the famous somersault type, designed by Edward French of Hitchin.

Single line block working was introduced on 28th March, 1877 using the train staff and ticket system. The staff for the Ayot to Harpenden section was a metal tube, approximately two feet long, with the centre flattened out in a diamond shape, and pink tickets were issued. For the Harpenden to Luton section the centre of the staff was crescent shaped and white tickets were issued. Tickets and wire hoops were kept in a large red box at each signal box. This system continued to be used until 20th March, 1955 when Tyer's single line subsidiary token system was adopted between Ayot and Luton East. From 25th August, 1957 the Hatfield to Ayot section was fully track circuited and worked as a tokenless section, based on the Direction Lever system. Chaul End became an intermediate block post on the Luton to Dunstable section on 18th December, 1955 - lineside token changing equipment was installed but this only survived until 5th June 1961.

On 23rd January, 1911 a new telephone system became operative using single needle conversing instruments, the circuit being Hatfield to Dunstable Church Street. This method remained in use until standard telephones were installed.

Hatfield No. 3 signal box controlled both the St Albans and Dunstable branches, together with Hatfield engine sheds, and at Twentieth-Mile Bridge there were signal boxes on either side of the lines - the down box controlling the Dunstable branch. However, this was closed when the new Welwyn Garden City signal box opened in 1926. This box controlled both the branch and main lines, although no connections were made between them. Extra levers were installed here to operate the passing loop which had been laid over a period of many months, but which eventually opened for freight trains in August 1958.

The up home signals at the foot of Ayot Bank were repeated by a banner repeater, because of the sharp curve in the track. The early lattice post of the down distant signal at Ayot was still standing, near the new upper quadrant

Hatfield No. 3 signal box seen from the Luton platform at Hatfield, with the site of the former locomotive shed on the left, *c.* 1963 *Photomatic*

Mrs Cox pulling the levers to control the crossing at Luton Hoo station.
Authors' Collection

signal, right up to closure of the line, as was the old up starting post. The down home signal was made upper quadrant, using the original post. Ayot's other signals were upper quadrants on tubular posts, with the exception of the up distant post which was concrete.

Before the loop was built at Ayot the signal box stood on the up side, opposite the platform, and comprised a brick base with wood and glass upper half, complete with fancy bargeboard and large finials, similar to the signal box at Harpenden. During 1892 the loop was installed, which necessitated the demolition of the old box. The new one, built of timber, stood at the Hatfield end of the new platform, and was approached by 12 steps. It contained a Saxby & Farmer 35-lever frame - the levers spaced at 4½ in. centres. This work formed part of a Contract between the Great Northern Railway Company and Saxby & Farmer in respect of signalling alterations to the branch, the bill for which totalled £3,144. Saxby & Farmer also supplied the shunting signals, which were the swivel type, but these were later modernised by having enamel discs fixed over the old faces.

The signal box at Wheathampstead was of timber construction and stood some 50 yards to the north of the station, overlooking the goods yard. Originally the signals were controlled from a lever frame at the north end of the station, almost immediately above the road bridge, but this was soon scrapped and replaced by the signal box. Fourteen steps led up to the box, which contained 18 levers. There were four signals in each direction; a distant and three stop signals. The signal box was closed in September 1921 when the points were connected to ground frames, which could be released by inserting the train staff.

The only signal at Leasey Bridge level crossing was a down distant which was connected to the gates, thus automatically indicating their position. This signal, a somersault arm, was mounted on a lattice post. As there were no signals for up trains engines whistled well before the crossing and again on approaching it. The crossing keeper was notified of approaching trains by the previous signal box.

Situated approximately halfway between Ayot and Luton, Harpenden naturally became the intermediate block post. The Harpenden signal box was able to switch out at night and weekends, and by switching out connected the long token section from Luton to Ayot. The signal boxes at Ayot and Luton had two sets of instruments, one for the long section and one for the short section. When Harpenden box was closed all trains ran over the down loop.

The up distant signal would only be pulled off when the signal box was closed and the stop signals off. The up outer home signal could be pulled off as normal, but the inner home signal had two levers connected to it, one for normal working and one which was operated when the box was closed. An

The driver of a dmu hands over the single line token to the Ayot signalman in 1965.

G. Goslin

Two class 'N7' 0-6-2Ts Nos. 69631 and 69698 leave Ayot station with a train to Hatfield on 2nd February, 1959.

A. Willmott

up starting signal was also provided on the down loop, but again this was only pulled when the box was closed.

The down distant signal was originally a sky-arm signal with the spectacle situated halfway down the lattice post. This signal and the down home were later replaced by upper quadrant signals, on their original posts. The down starting signal post was concrete and the advance starting signal post consisted of four metal tubes strapped together. Both signals had somersault arms.

Several changes took place in the signalling of the up line around the end of World War I. The up outer home signal was installed about 1921 and the up distant signal, which was then situated just north of Westfield Bridge, was moved approximately a quarter of a mile further along the line, thus enabling trains to come from Luton while shunting was in progress at Harpenden.

The up starting signal was at first situated to the south of the platform, but when the loop was extended to take 40 wagons, this signal was dismantled and a new one erected at the south end of the extended loop. The new signal had two co-acting arms on a concrete post. However, when the signal was renewed as upper quadrant it was repositioned on the site of the original signal. One of the early Saxby & Farmer swivel shunting signals remained in the yard until about 1950, when it was replaced by a standard disc signal.

The up distant signal had a tubular post and the outer home a tall lattice post. The inner home signal once had two co-acting arms on a 50 ft high lattice post, but in 1921 this was replaced by a single arm on a concrete post.

The signal box at Harpenden East contained a 30-lever frame, made by McKenzie & Holland, the levers being spaced at 6 in. centres, making a very long frame. It was a very spacious box, with a cupboard along the full length of the back wall and a large range stove in the fireplace, set across the corner. A token instrument was installed at either end of the signal box. At one time the steps up to the box were attached to the side wall and rose from rail level, but later a landing was added, from which steps descended to platform level.

Luton Hoo had a signal box until about 1930, when it was replaced by a ground frame. The box was sited to the north of the level crossing and was of timber construction, but the ground frame which replaced it was installed to the south of the crossing. The box contained an 18-lever frame and access was gained via 14 steps. The siding points were controlled by separate ground frames. At this time there were two entrances to the sidings, known as top and bottom points. Prior to 1930 there were four signals on the down side; the distant, a home and starting signal protecting the level crossing, and an advance starting signal beyond the sidings. On the up side were a distant and home signal protecting the level crossing and a starting signal beyond

A view of Welwyn Garden City station in 1921 showing the 20th Mile signal box up distant signals. *D. White*

Harpenden East signal showing a different style signal post to the signal on the right. *Authors*

Chaul End, 1947 photographed from the train. *G. Goslin*

the crossing. When the ground frame came the signals were reduced to a home and distant signal in each direction. In latter days the distant signals were renewed to upper quadrant on tubular posts, but the home signals remained with somersault arms on concrete posts.

Luton, being a more complex station, at first had two signal boxes - the East and the Yard - but on 10th September, 1899 a new one was opened at Luton West. This was of Great Northern character, timber-built and contained a 30-lever frame at 4 1/2 in. centres. Some time later the (West) up distant signal was changed from being a fixed signal to a working signal and an additional lever added to work it. The sidings were controlled by ground frames prior to the new box becoming operational.

Extensive signalling alterations were carried out during 1891, including the scrapping of the original East box and the opening of its replacement on the 16th March. It was at this time that the down inner distant signal was removed and the outer distant became a fixed signal because all trains stopped at, or in the vicinity of, the station. All the signals worked from the East and Yard signal boxes were, in the first instance, of the somersault type, but were later replaced by upper quadrant signals. Somersaults controlled from the West box remained right up until closure of the box on 15th December, 1969.

In the years following World War II Luton East signal box was well known because of its tilt towards the line, but whether this was due to the fact that it was constructed on built-up ground or to the bomb which fell in Midland Road during the war is not known. According to the signalman on duty at the time, the bomb-blast shook the signal box and disturbed every speck of dust in it, ruining the dinner he had just prepared! In time the box tilted so far that it had to be demolished, but first a new one was built alongside, to British Railways standard design, with 30 levers, and opened in April 1960. It carried the name Luton (Bute Street) East.

The section between Luton West signal box and Chaul End level crossing signal box was worked by a token. The small timber box at Chaul End contained a 10-lever frame. The level crossing was protected by a home and distant signal in each direction, the homes being somersault signals and the distants being upper quadrant. The down home signal had a banner repeater giving advance warning of its position. The points into Laporte's Chemical Works were controlled by ground frames released by the token.

When the new Dunstable North station was built by the London & North Western Company, the Great Northern Company closed the box at Dunstable Church Street and built a new one just east of Watling Street bridge, i.e. almost the furthest point of their territory. During demolition of the old box in January 1869 a Great Northern labourer and his friend were brought before the Justices for stealing eight shillings' worth of lead from its roof.

In 1890 the platform at Dunstable Church Street was lengthened and a new signal box erected, together with new signals. The points into the sidings were connected to this box, which was opened in November, but prior to this were connected to a ground frame. The box remained in use until 22nd July, 1934.

The London & North Western signal box at Dunstable North was sited to the west of the station beside the level crossing, and in later days took over the work of the two Great Northern boxes. British Railways replaced this signal box by a new one on the opposite side of the line, of standard design, with a 50-lever frame, which was opened on 16th August, 1958. All the signals at Dunstable North were upper quadrant on tubular posts, except the down distant from Leighton Buzzard which was a concrete post, and one other which was lattice. The sidings into Waterlows and the cement works were released by the token and electric lock from the signal box.

Dunstable North represented the end of single line working from Hatfield and as the signal box was a considerable distance from the station the single line block instruments were housed in the station buildings. When Chaul End signal box was switched out a long section was switched in from Dunstable to Luton West. It should also be noted that traffic on both branches ran 'down' to Dunstable ('up' to Hatfield and Leighton Buzzard). Between Dunstable North and Leighton Buzzard the line was double track controlled by absolute block working, a system introduced on 18th January, 1886 to replace the 'time interval' method of working.

Beyond Dunstable, the next signal box was at Forders Siding. Opened in 1886 and closed on 29th March, 1938, this box controlled the sidings which served chalk pits. At Gowers Siding there was a small signal box of London & North Western origin, opened in 1933, which contained 7 levers. Approached by three steps, it controlled access to sidings from the chalk quarries, only being used as required, although it was a block post. The signals were all upper quadrant.

Within half a mile of Gowers Siding was Stanbridgeford. Here a London North Western lever frame, mounted on the up platform, controlled the upper quadrant signals. The level crossing was hand operated but could be locked from the lever frame.

At Billington Road crossing all the signals were upper quadrant on tall posts, as were most of the others from here to Leighton Buzzard. The 6-lever frame controlling these stood in the open on the up side of the line but did have a hut beside it for the gatekeeper, in which were housed the signal repeater and track circuit indicators.

Grovebury Crossing signal box was a fine example of a London & North Western box, being kept in very good condition right up until closure. An

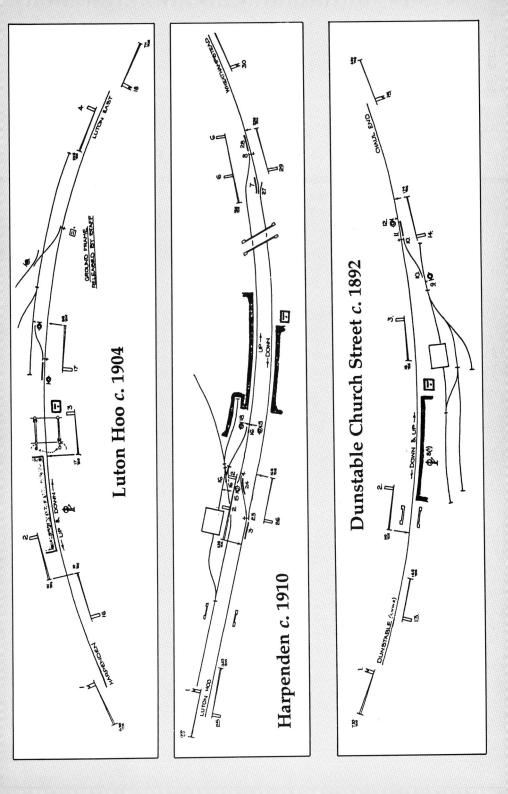

Luton Hoo *c.* 1904

Harpenden *c.* 1910

Dunstable Church Street *c.* 1892

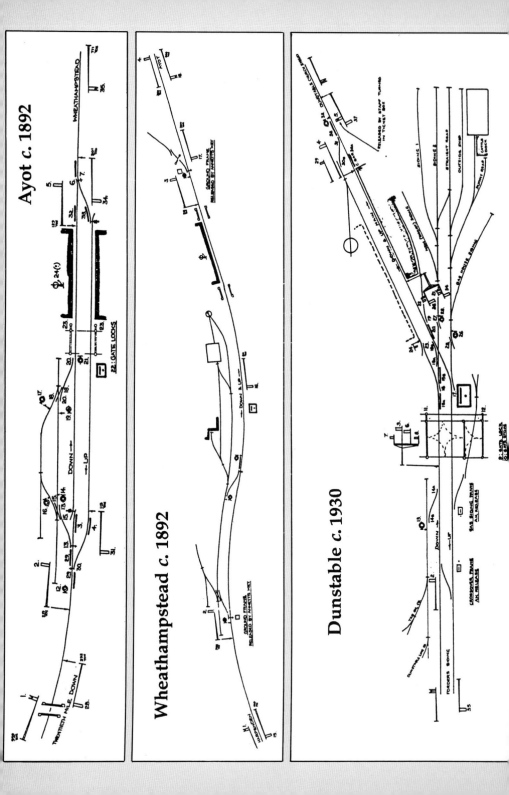

Ayot c. 1892

Wheathampstead c. 1892

Dunstable c. 1930

A GNR lever operated gong situated at the north end of the Luton line platform at Hatfield station, 1963.
Photomatic

Down home signals at Luton West seen in 1971; note the concrete post.
Authors

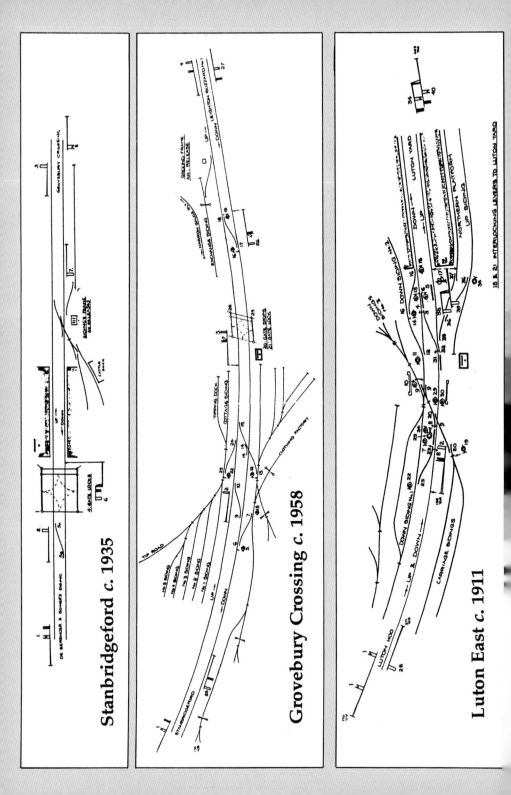

Stanbridgeford *c.* 1935

Grovebury Crossing *c.* 1958

Luton East *c.* 1911

sure. Ledburn Crossing signal box was not so fortunate and was in a very poor condition when it was 'retired' a few years before closure of the line. The home signals were then converted to fixed distants and the train crews had to operate the gates manually. The coal yard ceased operations at the same time.

Wing Crossing signal box, again of London & North Western origin, the last box before the main line, controlled a busy crossing over the A418 road. This box retained much of its old character, the inside being dark and old-fashioned with a quaint stove and oil-lighting. The lever frame, although constructed to accommodate 15 levers, in fact contained only five.

Chalk trains from Gowers Siding usually consisted of about 40 loose-coupled mineral wagons and as a result of some wagons breaking away on the 1 in 80 incline up to the main line, which ran back and crashed through the crossing gates, a special block bell code and regulations were applied. The most important point was that the Wing Crossing signalman must not re-open the gates for road traffic until the train had topped the incline and was acknowledged from Leighton Buzzard No. 2 signal box as being complete.

Access to the main line from the branch was controlled by Leighton Buzzard No. 2 box to the north of the station. When the main line was electrified and colour light signals were installed Leighton Buzzard No. 1 box was abolished on 4th July, 1965. No. 2 box remained, but only for shunting the few trains which used the branch, and was renamed Leighton Buzzard Shunting Frame. The main line resignalling gave the branch its only colour light signals, being the ones protecting the main line.

BRITISH RAILWAYS		BR. 2967A

TELEPHONE CIRCUIT CARD

HATFIELD - DUNSTABLE

Stations in Circuit	Call Signal
Hatfield Tele.Off.	••• •••
• Inspector	••••••
Welwyn Gdn.City Box	• ••••
Ayot Box	• • •••
Wheathampstead Tkt.Off.	—
Harpenden Box	•• •••
Luton Hoo Tkt.Off	••• ••
• • East Box	•• •
• Bute St.Inspector	•• •••
• Goods Office Exo	••
• West Box	••••
Laportes Siding	No call
Chaul End Box	- -
Luton Cold Storage Sdg.	No call
Dunstable Town Tkt.Off.	•• ••
Waterlows (Ldn.Rd.) Sdg	No call
Dunstable North Box	•••• •
BRIDGE. SITE	—

◊ Switch to Local Circuit

NOTE
Before ringing up a Station take the Receiver off and ascertain whether the Circuit is engaged. The Dot - represents a short ring and the Dash—a long ring.

GNR 4-4-2 No. 252 on an up Sheffield express just south of Hatfield station.

Real Photographs

GNR 0-4-2 No. 570 on a local service to Luton at Hatfield station.   *Real Photographs*

Chapter Four

Timetables and Trains

When the Luton to Dunstable section opened in 1858 the service consisted of five trains each way, running on weekdays only. Two of these trains were later sent through to Leighton. At this time the Luton Company had to hire trains from the London & North Western Railway Company, although they did employ their own station staff. On 1st December, 1858 a third train was scheduled to continue through to Leighton.

The Great Northern Railway Company took over the whole section between Hatfield and Dunstable when the new line was built and was, therefore, responsible for working it, although occasionally some LNW engines still ventured through to Luton. Hatfield shed provided the locomotives for the branch but sometimes Kings Cross engines ran through. An engine shed was built at Luton, though only used as a store in later years. Luton station served as the watering point, with water columns at the ends of the platforms.

With the opening of the Luton to Welwyn Junction section a Sunday service was inaugurated between Hatfield and Dunstable North, but this was cut back to Dunstable Church Street as from 1st June, 1866, because the London & North Western Company decided to close its North station on Sundays. This meant that Great Northern engines were unable to reverse, using the facilities at Dunstable North, and so alternative ways had to be found. When passengers had alighted at Church Street station the train went back about a quarter of a mile towards Luton, on a slight incline. When the guard had applied the brake he uncoupled the train from the engine, which then ran into the sidings, and whistled. On receiving this signal the guard released the brake, allowing the coaches to run back towards the station. The engine then emerged from the siding ready to rejoin its train to Hatfield.

To coincide with the opening of the Great Northern section, the LNWR increased its passenger service from four to nine trains each way, and in January 1866 admitted third class passengers. In 1864 the Great Northern timetable indicated seven down trains and six up trains on weekdays between Hatfield and Dunstable, with the London & North Western running connections from Dunstable to Leighton. Stops were made at New Mill End, Harpenden and Wheathampstead by request. At that time two trains each way ran on Sundays on the Great Northern section. By 1887 the service had increased to eight trains each way on weekdays, but still only two on Sundays.

When the Midland Railway came to Luton a better understanding developed between the London & North Western and Great Northern Companies

An up express hurries through Leighton Buzzard passing the Dunstable train; class '3' 2-6-2T No. 84002 on the right in August 1961. *Real Photographs*

Taking water at Leighton Buzzard. The locomotive shed is on the left.
Authors' Collection

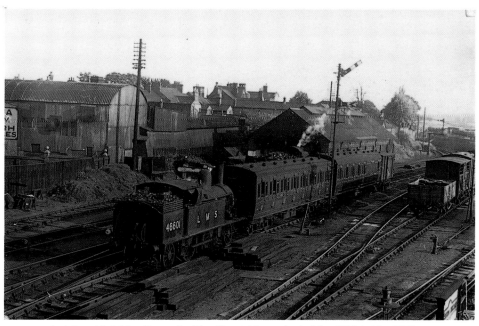

Arriving at Leighton Buzzard with a Dunstable service in May 1949, is No. 46601.

H.C. Casserley

No. 84002 again at Leighton Buzzard in August 1961 with a train from Dunstable.

Real Photographs

A Leighton Buzzard train leaving Dunstable North, 1960 . . . .   *H. Ramsey*

. . . . whilst another arrives in 1959.   *A. Willmott*

(probably in an effort to fight the competition) with the result that from 1st April, 1881 LNWR trains sometimes worked through to Luton. From 1st March 1883 trains ran from Luton to Leighton and on to Bletchley, via the newly installed connection, thus enabling them to compete with the Midland Railway for London to Luton and Birmingham traffic. Unfortunately this proved unsuccessful and trains were cut back to Leighton in November 1884.

It was only to be expected that the coming of these railways was considered an advantage not only to commerce and industry, but also to the general public, whose adventurous spirit led them to use the trains for excursions and Bank Holiday travel. On Good Friday 1886, 500 Lutonians bought tickets to Dunstable and 200 travellers went to other stations from Luton. On Easter Monday between seven and eight hundred people went to Dunstable, 100 to Harpenden and Ayot, while 300 joined an excursion to the Crystal Palace.

The GNR organised many excursions, as did the local Temperance Societies. A Luton gentleman, T.G. Hobbs, being a keen traveller, was always willing to try something different, with the result that one of his various excursions left Luton for Llandudno on Tuesday, 13th July, 1886, at 4.40 in the morning!

Seaside excursions were always very popular and the Great Northern often laid on trains to such places as Skegness, Hunstanton and Yarmouth. A report of one such trip was given by the Chairman to Great Northern shareholders stating 'although we got the people to Skegness alright, we could not get them away like clockwork. Some people were rather later getting to bed than usual but it was a beautiful day and no doubt all the people enjoyed themselves very much'.

An amusing story is told of a gentleman who had booked to join one of these excursions. Being a man of modest means, the forthcoming trip was something of a great occasion so, determined not to be late for the train, he decided to sit up all night, dressed and at the ready, bowler hat in hand. Unfortunately, sleep overtook him in the early hours and, living within earshot of Luton Hoo station, he awoke just in time to hear his train leaving.

Passenger traffic steadily increased, due to the lack of road competition, so that by 1900 nine trains ran in each direction daily between Luton and Hatfield. On the Luton to Dunstable section there were eight local trains and on the Dunstable to Leighton Buzzard line there were seven in each direction. The Great Northern Sunday service comprised two down trains, plus two early morning 'locals' between Luton and Dunstable (Church Street), and three up trains together with two 'locals' between Dunstable and Luton.

Around the turn of the century the GNR allowed horsecabs to use the forecourt of Luton (Bute Street) station, provided the proprietors had first obtained permission from the company - an innovation which benefited travellers and cab-owners alike.

Even though the Midland Railway took a direct route to London, there were times when the Great Northern route compared favourably. For example, a businessmen leaving work in London at 6.30 pm had a choice. Either he could take a Midland train which stopped at all stations and took an hour and a quarter to reach Luton, or he could take an express at 7 pm from Kings Cross for Hatfield where connection was made with a train for Luton. Even after a wait of six minutes at Hatfield the train arrived in Luton at 8.06 p.m. That particular express was a most punctual train - possibly due to the fact that the Prime Minister, Lord Salisbury, often travelled on it to Hatfield! For earlier travellers, the 4.30 pm train from Kings Cross ran to Hatfield, where it was divided - one part going to Hertford and the remainder to Dunstable.

During early years coaching stock was supplied from Kings Cross suburban area, comprising four- or six-wheeled coaches, of all classes. Second class accommodation was withdrawn from the Great Northern section from 1st November, 1891 and from the London & North Western section from 1st October, 1911. By 1913 the railway was enjoying a boom in passenger usage and it became necessary to run 10 trains each way between Hatfield and Dunstable on weekdays. However, a decision by the LNWR to reinstate a Sunday service on its section for a short period between 5th July, 1914 and 4th April, 1915, on an experimental basis, proved not to be a paying proposition - only 43 passengers used it on the first of those Sundays.

By contrast, the Great Northern staff were guaranteed a busy time when Harpenden's annual horse races came round. Special trains were arranged and Harpenden East station was turned into a centre of excited activity with passengers and horses arriving from far and wide, including London and Newmarket. These races, which were held on the Common, provided one of the most important social gatherings of the area and it was said that every thief and pickpocket in London was to be found in Harpenden that day! Unfortunately the outbreak of World War I put an end to the races.

It was around this time also that Gresley introduced his articulated coaching stock and these took over the majority of the workings, in pairs or multiples, on the Hatfield to Dunstable branch, right up until the start of railcars. Occasionally when there was a shortage of Gresley stock, main line corridor coaches were 'imported' for branch line work.

Just prior to, and during, World War I Hatfield was using Stirling-built 2-4-0 engines, Nos. 752/6 and 1066, 0-4-2 Nos. 25A and 592A, to work the branch, together with Nos. 1, 2 and 3 of his mixed traffic 0-6-0s of 1908 and one or other of his first 4-4-0s, Nos. 1072/8/80.

Up until this time a variety of engines had found their way onto the line, the earliest of which were some 2-2-2Ts converted from Sharp single-driving wheel tender engines of 1852. In the 1880s and 1890s the branch engines were Stirling rebuilds of outside-framed Sturrock 2-4-0 and 0-4-2 tender engines, such as 2-4-0 No. 253 (1866) and No. 102A (a Stirling rebuild of an 1848 Sturrock 0-4-2). These were followed by early Stirling designs of 2-4-0, such as Nos. 96 and 99 from the 1879 batch, with No. 11 (one of his first 0-4-2 engines, still running with its 4-wheeled tender) and 0-4-2 No. 10 of 1887. Tank engines at the time included 0-4-2WT Nos. 271/5 and 242A, this latter being a Stirling rebuild of a Sturrock 1865 0-4-2T. Engines of a similar period were used for goods traffic, for example 0-6-0 No. 449 of 1866, one of a batch originally destined to receive a tender.

By 1920/21 Gresley was able to introduce some much-needed suburban tank engines to take the place of the 4-4-2T class which, with Ivatt 0-6-2T 'N1s', were then toiling with the increased loads of the suburban stock. This in turn caused considerable alteration to Hatfield engines working on Luton trains. Consequently, with the arrival of the new 'N2' class all the 4-4-2Ts were moved away from London. For a brief spell during the transitional period, and prior to going north, Hatfield saw Nos. 1505/08/09/12/14/31/44 doing duties, with a final allocation, which lasted some years, of Nos. 1534/37/41/48 and 1550.

By 1921 the 0-4-2s had gone but 2-4-0 Nos.752 and 1066 lasted until April of that year when, London having absorbed all it wanted, sent some of the last batch of North British Locomotive Company-built 'N2s' Nos. 1759/60, 1763/67 and 1770 to Hatfield. A few were soon recalled but the remainder worked the branch, not always happily since they proved too heavy, especially at Dunstable LNW.

Goods engines employed at this time were mainly older Stirling designs, such as Nos. 101 (1881), 717 (1882) and 384 (1900), all having been rebuilt with domed boilers. On lighter duties the following engines were seen: the pioneer 0-6-2T No. 190, Stirling 0-4-4T No. 770 (now with domed boiler) or 0-4-4Ts Nos. 767 and 931, still with Stirling boilers and recently released from carriage pilot duties at Kings Cross.

By January 1924 a partial replacement of the 'N2s' began, Hatfield being sent 'N1' 0-6-2T Nos. 1560/64/69 from the Leeds/Bradford area, but they did not stay long, being replaced in July of that year by newly built 'N7' class 0-6-2T Nos. 933/4/5E from Stratford. Also at this time, Ivatt class 'D2' 4-4-0s worked the first morning train from Dunstable through to Kings Cross and in the evening worked the 5.49 from Kings Cross back to Dunstable.

After World War I ended the railway companies gradually got back to running excursions, and in July 1921 the Great Northern offered an 8-day excursion to Yarmouth and Lowestoft - although to take advantage of this offer holidaymakers had to leave Dunstable Church Street at 5.55 am. When the Great Northern Railway Company passed into the control of the London & North Eastern Railway one of the first excursions advertised was a day trip

The SBLC 'Banburian' special train at Luton Bute Street on 22nd September, 1962.

K. Taylor

GNR No. 1247 leaving Luton in April 1962. K. Taylor

A push-pull train to Leighton Buzzard leaving Luton Bute Street in 1962. Note the enormous GNR goods warehouse on the left. K. Taylor

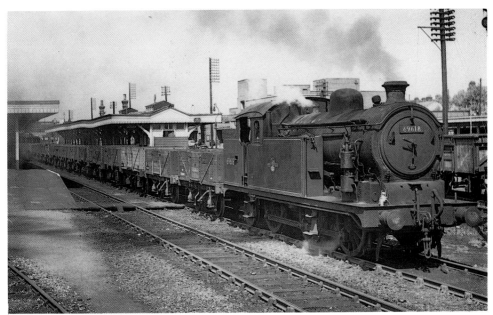

Class 'N7' 0-6-2T No. 69618 trundles through Luton Bute Street station with an up goods train. *Photomatic*

Class '4' 2-6-0 No. 43088 bound for Tottenham with a football special on 14th March, 1959. *S. Summerson*

GNR 0-4-4T No. 655 standing in the locomotive yard at Hatfield with the signals behind controlling access to the Luton and St Albans branches. *W.J. Reynolds*

Class 'J52 GNR 0-6-0T No. 1247 at Hatfield station on 14th February, 1962.
Real Photographs

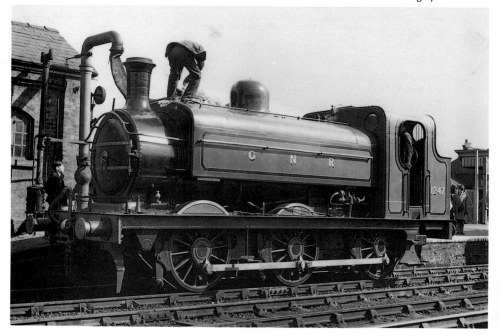

to London, offering possibilities of visits to the circus at Crystal Palace or
Olympia, the World's Fair at the Agricultural Hall or the 'Model Engineer'
Exhibition at the Royal Horticultural Hall. A number of excursions started
from Ayot, one of which, in August 1929, left at 6.44 am for Clacton, the third
class return fare being 8s. (40p). Some excursion handbills showed first class
fares (usually double the amount of the third class fare), but on the 6th
October, 1941 first class accommodation was abolished on the entire LNER
suburban service.

During World War II the service was reduced on the branch; in 1942 the
weekday timetable between Dunstable and Hatfield comprised seven down
trains with three locals between Luton and Dunstable, and seven up trains,
the first two of which went through to Kings Cross. Four locals ran from
Dunstable to Luton, but as for many years past, there were still only two
trains each way on Sundays. At Luton, during 1944, shunting was handled
by a 'Y3' class 0-4-0 Sentinel and, after the war, in 1946, two more 'Y3s', Nos.
8172 and 8175, arrived but were soon replaced by class 'J68' 0-6-0s, Nos. 8565
and 8572, which remained until 1952 when 'N2s' and 'N7s' took over the
day-to-day running of the line. In June 1947 a Great Northern saddle tank
(No. 8828) arrived in Luton for shunting duties and 'J3' 0-6-0s were occasionally seen heading ballast trains.

Following the war, nine up trains and seven down trains were timetabled
on weekdays and this service remained in operation until closure of the line
in 1965, with the exception of the Sunday service which was withdrawn on
the 21st January 1951. The only time the service was affected was during the
footplatemen's strike of May 1955 (when most NUR enginemen stayed at
work), resulting in a half-service being run.

Meanwhile, on the Leighton Buzzard to Dunstable section, 0-6-0 and 0-6-2
tanks hauled most of the passenger trains, which were usually push-and-pull
units, including No. 58926 (withdrawn in 1955 after 72 years in service) and
No. 58887. These were replaced by Ivatt and British Railways class '2' 2-6-2
tanks, including Nos. 41222 and 84002. More powerful engines were
required to enable freight traffic to climb the steep inclines at either end of
the branch. These were mainly ex-LNWR class 'G2' and 'G2a' 0-8-0 tender
engines, including Nos. 48930, 49094 and 49403, and latterly Stanier class '5s'
and '8s' with, occasionally, a Fowler '4F' in evidence. Servicing facilities
were available at Leighton Buzzard locomotive shed, but this closed on 5th
November, 1962.

As time went by the branch began to compete with road transport, but
there was still a demand for excursions. Mr Lee, for many years station master at Wheathampstead, and a revered member at the Parish Church, organised parties of Sunday School children and local residents onto special trains
bound for the coast. Besides giving the children a great deal of pleasure, the

trips provided a cheap day out for parents.

During the 1950s several special trains were run for the employees of Vauxhall Motors and their families to the circus at Olympia, London. The empty coaches started from Willesden, went to Leighton Buzzard and five vehicles continued to Luton via the branch (this being the maximum capacity for Sewell incline). At Luton Bute Street the two engines ran round the train and set off back to Leighton Buzzard, picking up passengers at all stations. At Leighton Buzzard these engines were taken off, seven more coaches added, and two 'Black Fives' or 'Jubilees' took the train to London.

In September 1953 a special train, organised by the Stephenson Locomotive Society and hauled by a Standard class '4' 4-6-0, No. 75034, passed along the line from Hatfield to Luton.

In February 1958 the decline in steam working began, when three diesel shunters (Nos. 3476, 3477 and 3478) were brought to Luton. These engines left Hatfield, where they were shedded, on Monday mornings and returned to Hatfield the following Saturday for maintenance and refuelling.

However, the steam engine was still very much in evidence on the branch and in April of the same year two notable engines appeared. The first, on the 18th, was a class '5' 4-6-0 No. 45195 (1E), which transported a crane to an industrial site adjoining the line, and the second, on 23rd April, was a class '4F' 0-6-0, No. 44397, from Bletchley which headed a weedkiller special. Weedkiller trains on the Midland section worked as far as Harpenden and then returned to Luton, and Eastern Region trains worked to Harpenden and returned to Hatfield - the boundary between the two Regions being marked by the down distant signal at Harpenden East.

The first occasion on which a Hatfield diesel worked beyond Luton was on 17th February, 1959, when a shunter, No. D2002, then in use at Luton, worked a freight train to Dunstable. On 15th June a Birmingham-Sulzer No. D5314, made its debut on the line, working the 6.07 pm down passenger train from Hatfield to Luton and Dunstable. It returned as a light engine, leaving Luton at 8.32 pm. The same engine hauled the 5.45 am passenger train ('the workmen's') from Dunstable North to Kings Cross for several days.

By September 1959 Hornsey Type 2 Diesels were responsible for working the 2.59 pm train from Luton to Dunstable North, returning with the 3.25 pm passenger train from Dunstable to Welwyn Garden City. In the evening an engine of this type worked the 7.30 pm from Welwyn Garden City to Dunstable, the eight coaches of which formed the first morning train to Kings Cross.

From this time on the decline in steam motive power was rapid, until by mid-1960 steam engines were only used to haul freight traffic. As from 6th June 1960 diesel locomotives of the English Electric type took over most of the passenger working. On 28th December Luton shunter No. D3490

STANBRIDGEFORD

The usual push-pull motor train to Dunstable seen here at Stanbridgeford station in
April 1962.   *Photomatic*

Shunting at Stanbridgeford in 1952.   *A. Willmott*

All previous issues cancelled.

No

G. N. R.

HALF-HOLIDAY EXCURSIONS.

Commencing 1st APRIL, 1909

(UNTIL FURTHER NOTICE).

CHEAP EXCURSION TICKETS

WILL BE ISSUED AS UNDER :—

EVERY WEDNESDAY & SATURDAY TO

DUNSTABLE
AND
HARPENDEN

RETURN FARES—THIRD CLASS.

	To Dunstable (Church St.)	To Dunstable (L. & N. W.)	To Harpenden
FROM LUTON	6d.	8d.	8d.

EVERY THURSDAY & SATURDAY TO

LUTON

RETURN FARES—THIRD CLASS

	From L & N W Station.	From Church St. Station
DUNSTABLE	8d.	6d.

Tickets will be available on day of issue only by any train after 12.0 noon

Children under 3 years of age, free; above 3 and under 12, half-fare. These cars are not transferable, and will only be available on the date of issue and at the stations named; if lost or at any other date, or at any other station than that named the holder will be charged full ordinary fare.

TICKETS, BILLS, and all Particulars can be obtained IN ADVANCE at the Booking Offices. For information respecting Excursions apply to J. HARDY, District Manager, G N Railway, Peterboro'.

London, King's Cross Station, March, 1909.

OLIVER BURY, General Manager.

W. & S. Ltd., D.

GREAT NORTHERN RAILWAY.

HALF-DAY EXCURSIONS.

EACH SATURDAY

COMMENCING JUNE 3rd, 1893,

and until 23rd September inclusive,

CHEAP HALF-DAY EXCURSIONS TO

ST. ALBANS,
WHEATHAMPSTEAD
AND
HARPENDEN

WILL BE RUN AS UNDER :—

	STATIONS	Time.	Fares for the double Journey, Third Class.	
			ST. ALBANS.	WHEATHAMPSTEAD HARPENDEN.
London	MOORGATE STREET dep.	2 15	2 0	2 3
	Aldersgate Street	2 17		
	Farringdon Street	2 19		
	KING'S CROSS (U.N)	2 40	1 9	2 0
	FINSBURY PARK	2 46		
	St. Albans aft.	3 24		
	Wheathampstead	3 32		
	Harpenden	3 37		

RETURNING ON DAY OF ISSUE ONLY

From HARPENDEN at 8.10 p.m. WHEATHAMPSTEAD at 8.24 p.m., and ST. ALBANS (U.N.) at 8.20 p.m.

Children under 3 years of age, free; above 3 and under 12 half-fare. Tickets not transferable.

Persons leaving excursion trains at intermediate stations further than those excursion tickets, and are required to pay the full ordinary fares.

Tickets available from King's Cross only, be obtained in advance at King's Cross Station; and at

HENRY OAKLEY, General Manager.

worked the 12.45 pm freight train from Luton to Leighton Buzzard, before it returned to Hatfield. With the closing of Hatfield shed on 2nd January, 1961 came the abolition of regular steam working, but steam engines were still used on occasional special trains, and a class 'B1' 4-6-0 usually hauled the breakdown crane.

A Metro-Cammell three-car multiple unit was tested on the Hatfield branch on 31st May, 1962 and these subsequently took over most of the passenger working, sometimes in two-car units or in multiples. In the same year, on 12th September, an Inspection Saloon arrived at Harpenden East from Leighton Buzzard, hauled by an Ivatt 2-6-0, No. 46431. After reversing, it returned to Leighton Buzzard. Meanwhile, during the 1950s only four trains were running each way on weekdays on the Leighton Buzzard to Dunstable section, and this service fell to three each way just before closure.

For a branch line of relatively minor importance, it was included in a good many excursion or special train routes, particularly during the early Great Northern days and again during the 1950s and early 1960s. At one time regular football specials were organised from Wolverton to Luton, via Leighton Buzzard, for Luton Town's home fixtures, and when the Club reached the semi-finals of the FA Cup in 1959 several specials came to Luton. One of these, from Ipswich, was hauled by an Ivatt 2-6-0, No. 43083. Later another football special, this time from Tottenham, came to Luton hauled by a Brush 'D56XX' class locomotive.

On Saturday 21st March 1959, the South Beds. Locomotive Club ran a special train, entitled 'The Skimpot Flyer', hauled by a 2-6-4T, No. 42467. It departed from Luton for Leighton Buzzard and after a round trip travelled back to Luton, via Hatfield and Ayot. The Railway Correspondence & Travel Society organised a tour, on 9th August 1959, known as the 'Grafton Tour', from Kings Cross to Leamington Spa and Banbury, returning to Leighton Buzzard from where the train travelled back to London via the two branches. The motive power throughout was Type 2 diesel, No. D6101.

The following year a tour, known as the 'Six Counties Limited', was arranged by the Locomotive Club of Great Britain on Sunday, 23rd April. The engine used for the last part of the trip was a Liverpool Street pilot, class 'N7' No. 69614, which worked down light in the morning to pick up the train at Leighton Buzzard. The tour left London (Paddington) in the morning and worked round to Leighton Buzzard for the return journey to Finsbury Park, via the Hatfield branch. On arrival at Leighton Buzzard the organisers of the tour observed that the engine was running bunker-first and requested it be turned. To achieve this, it had to be run to Bletchley, with the result that it commenced the last part of the journey some 25 minutes late.

Another trip between Hatfield and Leighton Buzzard formed part of a tour by members of the Branch Line Re-invigoration Society on 25th February,

1961. Rather than chartering a special train, they travelled on scheduled service trains, leaving Kings Cross at 11.30 am and going on to two other branch lines, at Northampton and Hitchin.

On 16th September, 1961 Captain Smith's class 'J52' locomotive, No.1247, resplendent in its Great Northern livery, worked a special train, under the title 'The Lea Flyer'. Organised by the South Beds. Locomotive Club, the 240 enthusiasts left Luton by a normal service train at 1.32 pm for Welwyn Garden City, where they joined the special train, driven by C. Winters of Hatfield, for the tour to Hertford and back to Hatfield, where the main line was crossed for the journey to Luton, arriving at 6 pm. This locomotive returned to the line on 14th April, 1962, and worked a Stephenson Locomotive Society special from Hatfield to Luton under the same title. A class '2P' 4-4-0, No. 40646, took over at Luton for the journey to Leighton Buzzard.

Owing to the decline in passenger usage of the Leighton Buzzard to Dunstable branch, notice was given that the passenger service would terminate as from 2nd July, 1962. Since there was no Sunday service the last train actually ran on 30th June, 1962. The final 'Dunstable Dasher' consisted of two well-filled coaches and was hauled by a steam engine, No. 41222 (the engine involved in the Skimpot blowback - see later chapter). Since very few official first class tickets were available most of the passengers had to be content with paper tickets.

Steam power was employed to haul a South Beds. Locomotive Society special on 22nd September, 1962 from Luton to Banbury, via the closed Leighton branch. The train was headed by an ex-LNWR class 'G2' 0-8-0 No. 48930, which left Luton at 2 pm and returned to Luton Midland Road station at 8.26 pm. The same society was responsible for the 'Cobbler Tour' on 19th September, 1964. This train left Luton at 1.50 pm and worked out to Leighton Buzzard and thence to Newport Pagnell, returning to Luton via the Midland line at 8.11 pm. The motive power was a class '4F' 0-6-0, No. 44414.

By the early 1960s passenger figures were falling, mainly due to an increase in private transport, with the result that the branch was one of many to fall victim to Dr Beeching's plan to 'axe' uneconomic lines. However, in the years leading up to closure an interesting selection of diesels had been implemented on both passenger and freight services, including classes 'D50XX', 'D55XX','D56XX', 'D65XX' and 'D8000' - all based at the Hornsey Diesel Depot, London.

Under Beeching's plan the passenger service was scheduled to be withdrawn on 6th January,1965 but several local councillors and other interested parties raised strong objections, forcing a reprieve, though only a temporary one, while the question of closure was reconsidered. One of the principal protestors was George Ausden, chief clerk at Bute Street station, who

An up train on the Luton branch between Luton Hoo and Harpenden seen here passing under the Midland main line on 2nd May, 1959.   *A. Willmott*

Picking up the single line token at Luton West signal box, *c*. 1950.   *G. Goslin*

EARL'S EASY BOOTS FOR THE EXCURSION.

GREAT TEMPERANCE EXCURSION
TO THE SEASIDE.

YARMOUTH
AND
CROMER,

ON WEDNESDAY JULY 9th, 1890.

The Luton and District Temperance and Band of Hope Union have made arrangements with the Great Northern Railway Company, and intend running a Special Train to those favorite watering places,

NUMEROUS ATTRACTIONS.

For the benefit of Friends and Bands of Hope connected with the Union, which appeals to them to avail themselves of this favourable opportunity

SPLENDID SANDS

FIRST CLASS BOATING, &c.

Arrangements have been made for issuing Tickets for One, Three and Four, Five or Seven Days. Parties of 8, by giving due notice to the Secretary, can secure reserved compartments

SEE OTHER SIDE FOR FARES.

The Secretary of each Society will be able to give all necessary information, and accept subscriptions from Children and Friends. The Excursion will leave Dunstable, calling at Luton 6.30 a.m., returning same day from Yarmouth (Vauxhall Station) at 7.30, from Cromer (Great Eastern) at 7 p m.

It is earnestly requested that an early application for Tickets be made to the following Gentlemen:—

Mr. W. ORD, 80, Chapel Street.
" J. GILLAM, 3, John Street.
" J. GILTROW, 37, Havelock Road.
" W. WALSH, JUN., 9, George Street, West
" J. DOCKRILL, Barbers Lane.
" H. BURNIT, 64, Collingdon Street.
" F. STRATFORD, 60, Langley Street.
And Hon. Secretary,
" W. H. COX, 57, Waller Street.

The Committee recommended HANNANTS, by 00A7R King Street, the Sec, for (Good Accommodation) on reasonable terms.

GEO. DALTON, Crown Printing Works. Luton.

EIGHT HOURS AT THE SEASIDE.

No. 1904.

G. N. R.

TERRITORIAL ENCAMPMENT

Saturday, November 28th, 1914.

EXCURSION TO

BURY ST. EDMUNDS

FROM	Departure Times	Return Fares Third Class
	a.m.	
DUNSTABLE {L. & N. W. Church Street}	11.25	
LUTON	11.30	3 3
HARPENDEN	11.50	
AYOT	12. 0	
HATFIELD	12.10	
WELWYN	12.20	
KNEBWORTH	12.30	3 0
STEVENAGE	12.38	
HITCHIN	12.43	
	12.54	
BURY ST. EDMUNDS arr	2.28	

Returning same day only from Bury St. Edmunds at 10.0 p m.

GENERAL CONDITIONS GOVERNING ISSUE OF THESE TICKETS.

The Company gives notice that these Tickets are issued at a reduced rate and subject to the condition that the Company shall not be liable for any loss, damage, injury or delay to passengers arising from any cause whatsoever.

CHILDREN under 3 years of age, free; above 3 and under 12, half fare.
TICKETS must be exhibited before joining the train or on demand during the journey, and delivered up at the end of the journey.
TICKETS are only available on the day and by the trains specified, and are not transferable.

For information regarding Excursions apply
G. MARSHALL, District Manager.
London, King's Cross Station, November, 1914.
C. H. DENT, General Manager

resigned that post in order to fight the proposed closure. Despite this campaign an Inquiry found in favour of withdrawal of the passenger service and this finally came about on 24th April. The last down passenger train was the 7.20 pm from Welwyn Garden City, consisting of a set of eight quad-arts coaches (Set No. 80) and hauled by a diesel Type 1, No. D8046, carrying a nameplate 'The Last Skimpot Flyer' (a nickname for the Luton to Dunstable trains brought about by the fast running along that section). It also carried a wreath from the South Beds. Locomotive Club. Small groups of onlookers gathered along the line but it was a very quiet farewell, apart from some detonators which had been placed on the line. The last up passenger train was the 7.35 pm from Dunstable to Hatfield, again hauled by a diesel Type 1, but this was almost empty, due possibly to the fact that prospective passengers found difficulty in arranging return transport.

So passenger carrying passed into the history books, but between Luton and Dunstable a goods service was still viable, so it was decided to put in a connection between the Midland main line and Luton East, in order to speed the dispatch of goods. Work started on this connection in November 1965 and it opened at the end of December, thus making the section between Luton (Vauxhall East Ground Frame) and Blackbridge Sidings redundant as from 1st January, 1966. On that date the goods service between Dunstable North and Grovebury Sidings was also withdrawn. This left three operational sections: Hatfield to Blackbridge Sidings, Luton East to Dunstable Cement Sidings and Grovebury Sidings to Leighton Buzzard.

In steam days Blackbridge-bound refuse trains were usually hauled by Austerity 2-8-0s to Hatfield, where 'N7' 0-6-2Ts took over. Before 1955 these trains ran through to Harpenden East, where the engine changed ends and pulled its train back to Blackbridge Siding, where it again reversed to propel its train into the siding. A brakevan was located at either end. Following withdrawal of steam in the Kings Cross area, trains were handed over to English Electric and Paxman Type 1 engines. By 1967 Blackbridge trains were the only Type 1 diagrams in the area and, following standardisation, Brush Type 2s took over to work the 1968/9 timetables.

On 20th March, 1968 'Baby Deltics', Nos. D5901 and D5904, in tandem, carried out loading tests on these trains with 41⅔ basic wagon units instead of the 48 allowed. Because of rough riding, Instanter couplings were used in the short position on most wagons (mineral and sulphate). However, it was found that with the 'Baby Deltics' length of 52 ft 6 in. as against the 42 ft Paxmans, difficulty would be found when a full load arrived on a following train. In consequence, one 'Baby Deltic', No. D5901, was used with a reduced load, but Brush Type 2s were again diagrammed for these trains. However, Nos. D8231/2/3 were usually employed to work the 1968/9

HITCHIN AND HERTFORD NORTH BRANCH

The Passenger Train Service on the above branch is cancelled

HATFIELD, LUTON AND DUNSTABLE BRANCH

DOWN WEEKDAYS

		2	3	4 Pass.		5	6	7	8	9	10		11	12	14
		Pass.	LMS Pass.	MX	MO	Pass.	Pass. SO	Pass.	LE	Pass.	Pass.		Pass.	Pass.	Pass.
		a.m.	a.m.	a.m.	a.m.	p.m.	p.m.	p.m.	p.m.	p.m.	p.m.		p.m.	p.m.	p.m.
Hatfield	dep.	7 32	..	8 20	8 20	..	12 48	2 5	4 50	..	4 56		5 43	6 48	7 42
Welwyn Garden City ..	,,	7 39	..	8 28	8 28	..	12 56	2 12	..	..	5A11		5 31	6 55	7 49
Ayot	arr.	7 44	..	8 34	8 34	..	1 2	2 17	4 11	..	5 16		5 37	7 1	7 54
,, ...	dep.	7 45	..	8 38	8 38	..	1 3	2 18	4 17	..	5 17		5 58	7 3	7 55
Wheathampstead ..	,,	7 51	..	8 45	8 45	..	1 10	2 24	..	..	5 23		6 5	7 10	8 1
Harpenden ..	arr.	7 56	..	8 50	8 50	..	1 15	2 29	4 28	..	5 27		6 10	7 15	8 6
,, ...	dep.	7 57	..	8 51	8 51	..	1 17	2 31	4 29	..	5 28		6 12	7 16	8 8
Luton Hoo	,,	8 3	..	8 57	8 57	..	1 23	2 37	..	..	5 35		6 18	7 23	8 14
Luton	arr.	8 9	..	9 3	9 3	..	1 31	2 43	4§40	..	5 42		6 26	7 29	8 21
,, ...	dep.	—	8 30	9 10	9 21	12 45	1 40	2 48	..	5 0	5 46		6 42	7 32	8 46
Dunstable Town ..	,,	..	8 40	9 22	9 33	12 54	1 50	2 58	..	5 9	5 56		6 54	7 43	8 58
Dunstable L.M.S. ..	arr.	..	8 43	9 27	9 38	12 59	1 55	3 2	..	5 14	6 0		6 59	7 46	9 7
Carriage Working No. ..	..	56	..	55	55	56	18	57	..	56	1		2SX 23SO	56	1

UP WEEKDAYS

		1	2	3	4	5	6 Pass.		8	9	10	11	13	15
		Pass.	Pass.	Pass.	LMS Pass.	Pass.	SO	SX	SO	Pass.	Pass.	Pass.	Pass.	Pass.
		a.m.	a.m.	a.m.	a.m.	a.m.	p.m.	p.m.	p.m.	p.m.	p.m.	p.m.	p.m.	p.m
Dunstable LMS ..	dep.	5 55	..	6 58	7 55	..	..	1 27	1 50	2 25	3 30	5 32	6 21	7 58	8 30
Dunstable Town ..	arr.	5 59	..												
,, ,, ..	dep.	6 0	..	7 3	7 59	..	..	1 31	1 54	2 30	3 35	5 37	6 26	8 2	8 34
Luton	arr.	6·10	..	7 12	8 8	..	..	1 40	2 3	2 39	3 44	5 46	6 35	8 11	8 44
,, ...	dep.	..	6 50	7 19	..	8 10	..	..	..	2 44	3 47	5 51	6 40	8 23	..
Luton Hoo	,,	..	6 56	7 25	..	8·17	..	..	..	2 50	3 54	5 57	6 45	8 29	..
Harpenden ..	arr.	..	7 1	7 30	..	8 22	..	..	..	2 55	4 0	6 2	6 50	8 34	..
,, ...	dep.	..	7 2	7 32	..	8 23	..	..	..	2 58	4 2	6 12	6 51	8 36	..
Wheathampstead ..	,,	..	7 8	7 37	..	8 29	..	..	..	3 3	4 8	6 17	6 56	8 41	..
Ayot	arr.	..	7 13	7 42	..	8 35	..	..	..	3 8	4 14	6 22	7 2	8 46	..
,, ...	dep.	..	7 14	7 46	..	8 36	..	..	..	3 9	4 15	6 23	7 4	8 47	..
Welwyn Garden City ..	,,	..	7 20	7 52	..	8 43	..	..	..	3 14	4 21	6 29	7 10	8 55	..
Hatfield	arr.	..	7 29	8 1	..	8 50	..	..	..	3 21	4 29	6 36	7 17	9 3	..
Carriage Working No. ..	..	57	25	26	..	57	..	56	56	18	37	56	1	56	2SX 23SO

DOWN SUNDAYS

			1		3	
			Pass.		Pass.	
			a.m.		p.m.	
Hatfield	..	dep.	9 30	..	7 40	.. ..
Welwyn Garden City	..	,,	9 37	..	7 47	.. ..
Ayot	..	,,	9 44	..	7 54	.. ..
Wheathampstead	..	,,	9 50	..	8 0	.. ..
Harpenden ..	..	,,	9 56	..	8 6	.. ..
Luton Hoo.. ..	..	,,	10 2	..	8 12	.. ..
Luton	..	arr.	10 9	..	8 19	.. ..
,, ...	..	dep.	10 14	..	8 24	.. ..
Dunstable Town ..	..	arr.	10 24	..	8 34	.. ..
Carriage Working No. ..		..	58	..	58	.. ..

UP SUNDAYS

			1		3	
			Pass.		Pass.	
			a.m.		p.m.	
Dunstable Town ..	..	dep.	7 12	..	6 16	.. ..
Luton	..	arr.	7 22	..	6 26	.. ..
,, ...	..	dep.	7 27	..	6 31	.. ..
Luton Hoo.. ..	..	,,	7 34	..	6 38	.. ..
Harpenden ..	..	,,	7 39	..	6Z44	.. ..
Wheathampstead	..	,,	7 45	..	6 50	.. ..
Ayot	..	,,	7 53	..	6 58	.. ..
Welwyn Garden City ..	..	,,	7 58	..	7 3	.. ..
Hatfield	..	arr.	8 5	..	7 10	.. ..
Carriage Working No. ..		..	58	..	58	.. ..

The passenger working timetable for 4th May, 1942 (until further notice) for the branch.

HATFIELD, LUTON AND DUNSTABLE BRANCH

SINGLE LINE (STAFF and TICKET). TRAIN STAFF STATIONS.—HATFIELD, AYOT, HARPENDEN, LUTON EAST, LUTON WEST BOX and DUNSTABLE (L.M.S.).

(LONG SECTION STAFF.—AYOT and LUTON EAST WHEN HARPENDEN CLOSED.)

Metal tickets with Annetts key attached are provided for the Harpenden and Luton East and Luton West and Dunstable L.M. & S Sections, for the purpose of unlocking the intermediate Siding connections. One engine in Steam Sundays, Luton West to Dunstable (L.M.S.).

Distance from Hatfield. M.	C.	DOWN.		WEEK DAYS. 21	23	24	25		26	27	28		29	30	32		33		34	35	SUNDAYS 11	12
				Gds.	Gds.	Gds.	Gds.		Gds.	Gds.	Gds.	Gds.	Gds.	Gds.	Gds.		Gds.		Gds.	Gds.	Gds. & Chs.	Gds.
		Class of train		B	B	B	B		D	B	D	D	D	B	D		B		B	B	B	B
				MX					K	Q	SX	SO								Q		
				a.m.	a.m.	a.m.	a.m.		a.m.	a.m.	a.m.	a.m.	a.m.	a.m.	p.m.		p.m.		p.m.	p.m.	a.m.	p.m.
...	...	HATFIELD	dep.	3 0	3E30	4 0	4 30	Dunstable Cement Siding arr. 7.28 a.m., dep. 7.40 a.m.	5 0	9 30	10 0	10 0	10 10	11 15	2 14	Dunstable Cement Siding arr. 4.40 p.m., dep. 5.0 p.m.	4 35	Dunstable Cement Siding arr. 9.38 p.m., dep. 9.58 p.m.	8 0	10 0	4 45	4 20
2	50½	Welwyn Garden City	,,	...	...	...	...		...	...	...	...	...	...	...		...		...	...	...	...
4	40¾	AYOT	arr.	3 15	3 45	4 15	4 45		5 15	9 45	10 15	10 15	10 45	11 30	2 29		4 50		8 15	10 15	5 0	4 35
			dep.	3 16	3 46	4 16	4 46		5 16	9 46	10 16	10 16	Horn's Siding arr. 10.20 a.m., dep. 10.40 a.m.	11 31	2 30		4 51		8 20	10 16	5 1	4 36
6	43¾	Blackbridge Siding	,,	...	Dunstable Cement Siding arr. 5.0 a.m. dep. 5.22 a.m.	...	...		...	...	...	...		...	...		...		...	...	...	...
7	30	Wheathampstead	arr.	...		Shunt Luton Coal Yard	...		5 24	...	10 24	10 24		...	2 38		...		...	...	...	...
			dep.	...			...		5 34	...	10 44	10 44		...	2 48		...		...	...	V	...
9	48½	HARPENDEN	arr.	...			...		5 41	...	10 52	10 52		12 0	2 56		...		8 35	...	...	...
			dep.	...			...		5 56	...	11 20	11 20		Blackbridge Siding Shunt.	3 18		...		8 36	...	V	...
12	0¼	Luton Hoo	arr.	...			...		...	...	...	...			...		...		...	...	...	...
			dep.	...		...	...		...	...	*	*			...		...		...	...	...	...
14	76	LUTON STATION	arr.	3 45	4E16	4 46	5 16		6 11	10 15	11 40	11 40			3 33		5 20		8 50	10 45	5 45	5 6
			dep.	Shunt Luton West End Sidings	4J40	...	6 10		7 10	...	12 50	...			3 55		...		9 20	...	6 20	5 26
15	6	LUTON WEST BOX ¶	arr.		...	...	...		...	...	Dunstable Cement Siding arr. 1.8 p.m., dep. 1.28 p.m.	...			...		...		...	...	...	...
			dep.		...	...	...		...	...		...	...		...		...		...	...	...	...
		DUNSTABLE Town	arr.		...	...	6 25		...	...		...	...		4 9		...		...	...	...	...
			dep.		Y	...	6 33		...	...		...	...	...	4 29		...		...	...	...	...
19	21	DUNSTABLE Ln. Rd	arr.		...	...	...		7 45	...		...	...	...	...		...		...	...	6 40	5 46
			dep.		...	...	...		...	...		...	...	...	...		...		...	...	...	...
20	30	DUNSTABLE L.M. & S.	arr.		5 25	...	6 38		...	...	1 31	...	...	...	5 0		...		10 1	...	...	...

E. On Mondays 23 down to have extra engine attached to Luton to shunt West End Sidings.

J. Conveys empty coaches.

K. Shunt Waterlow's Siding and work coaches from Dunstable LMS to London Road off passenger due Dunstable, L.M.S. 9.38 a.m. M.O.; 9.27 a.m. M.X.

V. Stops to leave newspapers.

Y. Stops at Bagshawe's Siding to attach and detach.

Distance from Dunstable. M.	C.	UP		WEEK DAYS. 21		22		23	23	24		24	25	26	27	28		30		31	32		SUNDAYS 11		12	
				Gds.		Gds.		Gds.	Gds.	Gds.		Gds.	Gds.	Gds.	Gds.	Gds.		Gds.		Gds.	Gds.		Gds.		Gds.	
		Class of train		D		D		B	B	D		D	D	D	B	B		D		B	D		D		D	
								SX	SO	SX		SO								Q						
				a.m.		a.m.		p.m.	p.m.	p.m.		p.m.	p.m.	p.m.	p.m.	p.m.		p.m.		p.m.	p.m.		a.m.		p.m.	
		DUNSTABLE L.M. & S.	dep.	...	Dunstable Cement Siding arr. 9.48 a.m., dep. 10.8 a.m.	10 25	Dunstable Cement Siding *	...	...	2 0	Dunstable Cement Siding arr. 2.5 p.m., dep. 2.25 p.m.	...	...	...	6 5	...	...	8 40	Dunstable Cement Siding arr. 8.43 p.m., dep. 9.3 p.m.	...	10 30	Bagshawes Siding arr 10.53 p.m., dep. 11.13 p.m.	...	Dunstable Cement Siding arr. 11.3 a.m., dep. 11.23 a.m.	...	Dunstable Cement Siding arr. 9.13 p.m., dep. 9.33 p.m.
		DUNSTABLE Ln. Rd.	arr.	...		...		...	...	...		...	...	...	...	...	...	...		...	10 33		...		...	
			dep.	9 45		*		...	...	...		...	...	...	...	...	...	...		...	10 48		11 0		9 10	
1	9	DUNSTABLE Town	arr.	...		...		...	...	...		...	...	...	...	...	...	...		...	11 17		...		...	
			dep.	...		...		...	...	...		...	...	...	...	...	...	...		...	11 27		...		...	
5	24	LUTON W. BOX ¶	arr.	...		...		...	...	...		...	...	...	...	...	...	...		...	...		...		...	
			dep.	...		...		...	...	...		...	...	...	...	...	...	...		...	...		...		...	
5	34	LUTON STATION	arr.	10 26		11 25		...	...	2 43		...	...	...	6 25	...	...	9 23		...	11 42		11 45		9 55	
			dep.	11 0		11 50		...	...	3 0		3 0	...	7 10	8 0	9 0	...	10 53		11 30	12 1		11§55		10 10	
8	29½	Luton Hoo	arr.	...		...		...	...	...		...	...	...	...	...	...	...		...	...		...		...	
			dep.	...		...		...	...	...		...	...	...	...	...	...	...		...	...		...		...	
9	30¾	Hyde Mill Siding	arr.	...		...		...	...	...		...	...	...	...	...	...	...		...	...		...		...	
			dep.	...		...		...	...	...		...	...	...	...	...	...	...		...	...		...		...	
10	61½	HARPENDEN	arr.	11 15		12 5		...	...	3 15		3 15	...	7 25	8 15	9 15	...	...		...	...		...		...	
			dep.	11 16		12 6		12 20	1 20	3 16		3 16	...	7 40	8 38	9 16	...	...		...	...		...		...	
13	0	Wheathampstead	arr.	...		...		...	...	...		...	...	*	...	...	...	...		...	...		...		...	
			dep.	...		...		...	...	...		...	...	...	...	...	...	...		...	...		...		...	
13	66½	Blackbridge Siding	,,	...		...	*	...	...	...		...	...	...	...	...	...	...		...	...		...		...	
15	69½	AYOT	arr.	11 30		12 19		12 35	1 34	3 31		3 31	...	8 15	8 53	9 31	...	11 25		11 59	12 31		12§24		10 40	
			dep.	11 31		12J20		12 36	1 35	3 32		3 32	6 35	8 20	8 54	9 32	...	11 26		12 1	12 32		12§25		10 41	
17	59½	Welwyn Garden City	,,	...		...		...	...	...		...	...	...	...	...	...	...		...	...		...		...	
20	30	HATFIELD	arr.	11 43		12J32		12 48	1 48	3 44		3 44	6 47	8 35	9 10	9 46	...	11 40		12 15	12 46		12§37		10 53	

¶ All engines and trains must stop at Luton West box for train staff or ticket purposes.
J. On Saturdays Ayot dep. 1.8 p.m., Hatfield arr. 1.20 p.m.

Freight working timetable for the branch, dated 22nd May-1st October 1944.

of service. D8232 was later reinstated.

Although it had been decided not to use 'Baby Deltics' on Blackbridge trains, the unusual combination of Paxman/'Baby Deltic' was occasionally used (as on 3rd November, 1969 with Nos. D8232 and D5905, and again on 23rd November). D8231 and D8232 were brought back again on 9th February, 1970 and remained until April, when D8232 went to the works for attention. From then on pairings using Nos. D8230, 8201, 8231 and Brush Type 2s were employed, until closure of the Dump on 24th May, 1971.

In October 1968 the Midland Railway London Extension Centenary Celebrations Association organised events at St Albans, Luton and Bedford. All Company rivalry forgotten, Bute Street Goods Yard was taken over by their Exhibition Train from the 11th-13th October (open from 10 am to 8 pm daily).

As part of the celebrations, a special diesel train ran from St Pancras to Bedford. The return train left Bedford at 4 pm and ran back to Luton, where it became the first passenger train to use the connection between Midland Road and Bute Street stations, to enable it to journey to Dunstable North and back again. To complete the tour the train made its way back to London, stopping at Harpenden Central and St Albans to set down passengers.

Punch Hull, 0-4-0ST, built by Andrew Barclay works as No. 776 and *Tom Parry*, 0-4-0ST also built by Andrew Barclay as works No. 2015, stand in their shed at Dunstable Cement works in 1966. Both were out of use by 1967.   *R. Flanagan*

Chapter Five

Travellers and Traffic

Although both branch lines could only be considered as small cogs in the whole railway machinery, they were honoured in the number of famous and noble travellers they carried. On 5th December, 1878 the Prince of Wales travelled to Luton Hoo House and afterwards visited several Luton hat factories, returning to London via Luton Bute Street station. He came back again, this time with his Princess, and stayed from the 7th-11th December, 1886. On leaving the Hoo they travelled to Luton so that the townsfolk could see them.

An agreement was reached between the Great Northern Company and Mr John Leigh of Luton Hoo whereupon trains were obliged to stop at New Mill End station when requested by him. However, the company refused to renew the agreement in 1861.

Another notable traveller was Mr George Bernard Shaw, who moved to Ayot St Lawrence near Wheathampstead in 1906. He often made use of the line to convey him to London, but had a bad habit of nearly always arriving late, making it necessary for his chauffeur to run on ahead to hold up the train until his arrival. Goods for Mr Shaw were collected from Wheathampstead station by Mr R.O. Catford, who owned a taxi firm in Ayot St Lawrence until 1928.

Unfortunately Mr Shaw's connections with the line were not always happy ones, for the rubbish dump at Blackbridge was a constant irritation to him because of the fumes which often drifted over to his house. In a letter to the council he wrote that he was reminded not of Shakespeare's 'thyme and violet scented bank, but of stromboli and hell!'. He felt that his near neighbour, Mr C. Cherry Garrard of Wheathampstead House (near the station) and survivor of the 'Worst Journey in the World' had 'suffered no more from the rigours of life at the South Pole than he had from the stench of that dump!' (From *Shaw - the Villager and Human Being.*) However, it does not seem there were any ill feelings between him and the station staff at Wheathampstead, because he usually sent them a card and a gift at Christmas.

An amusing incident concerned a horsedealer from the Wheathampstead district who was a regular traveller, known to passengers and staff alike. One day a new ticket collector asked to see the man's ticket. This unexpected request caused the gent to explode with the cry 'My face is my ticket'. 'Ah well' replied the ticket collector, 'my instructions are to punch all tickets'!

No doubt there were many regular travellers but one of special note must be a Mr Fletcher of Luton who held a season ticket for 52 years. Unlike him, there were many who made occasional journeys, particularly during the

Luton GNR station at Bute Street with the Midland main line in the background.

Authors' Collection

Hatfield station buildings photographed in 1963.   *Photomatic*

'N7' class 0-6-2T No. 69692 waiting at Welwyn Garden City station on 8th August, 1959.   *S. Summerson*

depths of winter when road transport could not be relied on. Mr J. Coe, a relief station master at Ayot could remember the waiting room being full of country gents' gum-boots, awaiting their owners' return.

Turning the clock back, the following letter, written by a Luton Quaker to his son at boarding school in Yorkshire, gives an idea of what travelling may have involved in the very early days of the branches, as it was dated 5th July,1861:

My Dear John,

I believe it will be two weeks tomorrow since thou had my last letter, in which I told thee we had fixed for thee to come home by Leighton. I cannot say yet whether any of us will be able to meet thee there. If thy Mother is at home she will most likely do so but if not thou must endeavour to manage thyself.

First take care and bring thy bundle out of the carriage thou leaves, then tell some of the railway people who are about that thou wants to go to Luton by the train which will start a few minutes after thou reaches Leighton. Thou wilt have to go down some stairs, then turn to the right, then up some more stairs and to the right again is the booking office where thou must ask for a 2nd Class ticket to Luton which will cost 1s. 6d. At Dunstable thou wilt have to change carriages, the Luton train will presently come up to the platform, when thou wilt get in and soon find thyself at Luton.

Mind and do not hurry to get in or out till the carriage is quite still they will not go without thee if thou uses thy tongue and says where thou art going.

Now I think I have told thee all I need do to get safely here if no one of us can go to Leighton to meet thee. Thou must ask T.P. for 1s. 6d. to get thy ticket at Leighton with, in case we are not there, unless they could book thee to Dunstable which they might do as it belongs to the North Western that far.

Thou must be careful not to rub thy face about with thy hands on the journey home so as to keep it clean and fit to be seen. Thou should get here a little before four on the sixth day as the Luton train leaves Leighton pretty soon after thy train comes in.

It seems this father took great trouble to explain to his son exactly what he must or must not do, for in 1862 he wrote again with the following instructions:

I hope thy ticket will book thee through to Luton, if it does thou wilt only have to change at Hatfield into a 3rd Class carriage there for Luton. The booking office at Hatfield is on the same side of the way as you get out the carriage. When thou crosses over to the Luton train mind not to go upon the rails - go over the bridge as there are express trains which run without stopping there sometimes.

Since the line meandered through countryside and cut through towns and villages it was only to be expected that a large number of varying commodities would be carried by the railway. Luton, being the largest town on the route, therefore became the centre of freight handling, particularly for coal and straw plait. The transportation of coal from South Wales was handled by the London & North Western as far as Dunstable North and then transferred to the Great Northern, who brought it through to Luton. The company also brought in coal from the north of England, via Hatfield, and on one occasion in June 1894 a surprise 'cargo' arrived in a wagon from South Yorks Collieries. It was a sparrow's nest, with four eggs, and the mother bird still sitting. Sadly, she was frightened away during unloading.

In 1906 a large coal yard was built to the south of Bute Street station and the site of the old coal yard was developed with a massive extension to the goods shed, costing £25,000. The extent of the new building could be clearly defined by the colour of the brickwork.

Luton, being the centre of the hat industry, received and dispatched goods by rail - the Great Northern carrying more than the Midland line around the turn of the century. Both lines had large warehouses to deal with the trade and in the evenings Bute Street was full of carts loaded with hat boxes *en route* to the stations, mainly destined for markets in London and Manchester. March, April, May and June were the busiest months, when there was plenty of overtime and more men, horses and drays had to be hired, besides the 18 or so which belonged to the Great Northern Company.

A mixed train left Luton at 8 pm nightly for destinations within LNWR territory, whilst Great Northern trains would leave at 8.40, 9.30 and 10.30 pm to convey hats to Kings Cross. Wagons for the north of England went by the 9.30 pm train and were shunted at Hatfield. On 20th April, 1898, a total of 756 boxes of hats were dispatched from Luton at 1.50 am (the delay due to the quantity to be loaded). Due to the vast quantity of boxes to be carried that night, and a shortage of goods wagons, two cattle wagons also had to be utilised.

Goods staff were able to leave work after the departure of the last train but started again at 6 am the following morning, unloading empty hat boxes, wool and straw plait from China, and generally preparing the vans for the next evening rush.

Complaints came quite regularly from the Luton Chamber of Trade regarding abnormalities in carriage rates between the two original railway companies, particularly for straw goods. However, on 16th May, 1887 the GNR and LNWR companies agreed on rates to Scotland, these being (per ton) Edinburgh and Glasgow 100s., Dundee 105s. and Aberdeen 110s. Prior to this agreement the rate had been 125s. to Glasgow and *pro rata* elsewhere. Needless to say, the new rates were welcomed by manufacturers.

Despite these disputes it would appear that relations between the hat manufacturers and the railway staff were quite amicable, as in 1873 Messrs Simpson, Waller and Cochin arranged a dinner at the Midland Hotel for

Great Northern employees in recognition of their 'uniform assiduity and punctual delivery' when dealing with an extra large importation of Canton plait.

One of the many perishable commodities carried was fish. It sometimes travelled in special wagons, but for speedier delivery came with passenger trains, though not always successfully. On 11th August, 1875 Mr Hammett, a Luton fishmonger, claimed damages of £3 5s. to a consignment of fish from Grimsby, which arrived 'fit only for soup'! It had been delivered to him in a sack, complete with the broken boxes, but the guard assured the Court that it had been in that state when he took charge of the goods at Hatfield. The case was eventually dropped.

The turn of the century saw the construction of extensive sidings to new factories adjacent to the line at Luton. One of the reasons for this sudden development, apart from the cheap land with rail access, was the supply of electricity which was available for working machinery cheaper and cleaner than steam power, which blackened so many northern towns at this time. The Electricity Company and their near neighbour, T. Balmforth & Co., boilermakers, who started in 1872, shared sidings from the new coal yard.

To the east of the coal yard, Messrs Haywood Tyler & Co., hydraulic engineers, built a factory in 1875, when they moved from Clerkenwell, and had a siding running into the works. It was known as 'the brass foundry' to distinguish it from Brown & Green's iron foundry, even though both concerns had an iron foundry and a white foundry. Behind Luton Yard signal box, a short siding served Gidding's stonemasons' yard.

The Vauxhall & West Hydraulic Engineering Company was founded by Alexander Wilson, principally for building steam engines for tugs and paddle boats. His company moved to a half-acre site in Luton in 1905 and employed 150 men, after the lease of their ironworks in London expired. They continued to produce marine engines until the Kaiser's War and in 1907 Vauxhall Motors Limited formed. They sent their cars by rail, sometimes complete, but usually in crates for export, travelling via Finsbury Park to Harwich. At peak times in latter years Vauxhall sent out two train-loads of cars per day, each comprising 40 wagons. Coal was taken into the company's sidings as fuel for its own gas-making plant, and waste materials were dispatched by rail.

During World War II steel sheets were made at Jack Olding's works at Hatfield, at which station they were loaded onto the railway and taken to Vauxhall for war vehicle production. In all 249,000 trucks, 5,640 tanks and 2,548 cars were made for the Ministry of Supply, many of which were transported by rail. A large number of tanks were taken as far as Ayot before going on by road to the Tank Corps at Hatfield House.

By 1965 the company employed 28,000 men in factories covering 420 acres

An undated view of a down train's arrival at the first Welwyn Garden City station.   *Authors' Collection*

Class 'N7' 0-6-2T No. 69698 seen here arriving at Luton Bute Street from Hatfield on 19th April, 1960.   *S. Summerson*

of land and a new factory had been constructed at Dunstable (between the Town and North stations). Access sidings were opened on 22nd October, 1956, but the new factory used these mainly for taking away swarf.

From time to time Luton Goods Yard played host to Exhibition Trains, one of the most popular being Fry's Show Train, which comprised three coaches and arrived on 7th January, 1937. Members of the public were encouraged to visit the exhibition (admission 2d.) where many natural history items were displayed and free samples of Fry's chocolates were distributed.

Luton West was the centre of another group of factories. Two sidings ran down into Henry Brown's Timber Yard and ended just short of Dunstable Road. An overhead gantry and a large crane were installed for unloading the timber. Close to this siding, another served the English & Scottish Joint Co-operative Wholesale Society Chocolate & Cocoa Factory, which opened in 1902.

Also on the down side from Luton West signal box a long siding ran beyond Clifton Road bridge into the factory of the Davies Gas Stove Co., iron founders and makers of gas apparatus, who came to Dallow Road, Luton in 1895 from Camberwell. Most of their staff hailed from Falkirk and their arrival in Luton caused a small social upheaval. On the other side, the small scrap yard owned by Cohen Ltd provided a small amount of traffic via Maple Road Coal Yard. In 1936 the Gas Works was built between New Bedford Road and Dunstable Road, into which ran two long sidings. A shorter siding ran back adjacent to these to serve Arnold's Timber Yard, facing onto New Bedford Road. It was this land that Tomson had bought for £200 per acre when the line was first proposed.

Laporte Chemicals came to Kingsway, Luton in 1898, making hydrogen peroxide for hat bleaching, but later made all forms of chemicals, bringing plenty of traffic to their sidings. Whilst only indirectly connected with the branch, this incident at Soham on the Ely to Newmarket line on 1st June, 1944 is thought worthy of inclusion. The driver of a munitions train looked out and saw the first wagon on fire. Acting with great courage, he separated the burning wagon from the rest of the train and took it forward. Seconds later it exploded, killing the driver and a signalman. It transpired that the wagon had been to Luton (Laporte) with a load of sulphur in bulk, and for some reason had not been cleaned out, with the result that a spark from the engine had ignited the powder which remained.

At Chaul End a factory was taken over for shell-filling as part of World War I effort. The women who worked there could easily be recognised by their orange-yellow faces, caused by the dust from the explosive powder. Here a temporary station had been opened in 1915, at which LNWR trains also called as from 28th February, 1916, but this closed in February 1920. A siding, of five wagons length, serving the factory closed on 20th April, 1916.

Close-by, and dating from 1840, was Brown & Green's iron foundry (makers of the ironwork for Skimpot Lane Bridge).

In 1892 B.J. Forder started a lime works at the foot of Blows Down, near Skimpot. It covered quite an extensive site and had sidings running alongside the kilns. Although it closed in the 1920s, parts of the kilns were still visible in the 1990s.

Dunstable, being a busy and productive town, made use of its rail connections, dispatching and receiving goods of all kinds. Perhaps the most unusual use the line was ever put to was the carriage of elephants and camels (and perhaps other animals), *en route* to Whipsnade Zoo for its opening in 1931. There arrival caused excitement and curiosity and many people turned out to see the animals, which then had to walk all the way from Dunstable North station to Whipsnade.

Returning to more mundane traffic, Dunstable Town received coal for local merchants and handled scrap iron (part of the goods yard was occupied by a scrap dealer). In 1906 a siding was constructed into Bagshawe's engineering works.

Between the Town and North stations Associated Portland Cement built its works in 1925, mainly because of its easy access to the chalk on the edge of the Chilterns, and was one of a line of four quarries; the others being at Sundon, Pitstone and Chinnor.

The sidings at the Dunstable works, which opened in October 1925, provided a triangle giving an east and west access. Both sides of the triangle consisted of two sidings, which joined into one to run round the works. A catchpoint was installed to prevent wagons stabled in the triangle sidings from running back down the gradient and into the works. To the eastern boundary were three long sidings, for storage, from which a spur ran down to the works. Originally, this gave only two loading sidings, from which the first cement left by rail on 10th September, 1926. The weighbridge, dating from 1926, was still in working order and tested in 1971. Later the sidings were extended to give more loading platforms and a double siding to a rail wagon loading hopper over the two lines, together with a short spur to the engine shed. On 9th June, 1936 an abnormal load, consisting of four large rotary kilns loaded on flat wagons, arrived at the works from the north of England.

With the introduction of new Presflo wagons and bulk tankers, a new loading hopper was built over the access line, giving space for loading or unloading two wagons at a time. Weighing was done at the same time. By Easter 1971 the older part of the works was out of use; although still in working order, it was too costly on manpower to be viable.

All points on the system were hand-operated as required and a sand drag was fitted near the catch-point to deal with runaways. Unfortunately trouble was caused by children interfering with the brakes of wagons and on one occasion two loaded wagons ran away, became derailed in the sand drag and overturned. Rerailing proved a somewhat tricky operation. It was eventually accomplished using spare sleepers, a jack and lots of grease! In an effort to reduce flange wear on the sharp curves, two automatic greasers were fitted to the rails, but the general opinion was that the £200 spent had not produced the expected results.

During the lifetime of the works several alterations were made to the track system, the work being carried out by Thos W. Ward, who also took up old railway lines. This probably accounts for the variety of chairs to be found there - some even found their way from the Cheshire Lines Committee.

Chalk was latterly carried the two miles from Sewell to Houghton Regis by pipeline, but this ceased early in the 1970s and the bridge carrying the pipe over the A5 road was demolished in January 1973. Cement was then brought in from Northfleet and the works used purely for storage and bagging, until July 1988 when the works closed.

At Dunstable North, known as the 'Lower Station', there were sidings serving many concerns. Opposite the Cement Works, Waterlows had a siding into their printing works. It was here that many railway advertisements and timetables were printed.

Between Waterlows and the Watling Street was the Great Northern Coal Yard, opened in 1885, and also the cattle dock, part of which was latterly used as an oil storage depot. The yard behind the North station (the site of the original London & Birmingham Company station) known as the LNWR Yard, was used for large quantities of coal and fertilizers, besides general traffic. William Lockhart operated from this yard, both as coal merchant and dealer in building materials.

The Gas Works, just north of the station, naturally received many trainloads of coal and dispatched by-products, usually in wagons owned by Midland Tar Distillers Ltd. It was formed as the Dunstable Gas & Water Company in 1871 and had a 77 ft-deep well, which served the town until the new one was sunk on Half Moon Hill in 1895.

Just beyond the level crossing a siding was laid about 1918 to serve the Dunstable Lime Company's new quarry at the top of Sewell Bank. From this siding ran two more, one into a barrel factory (nicknamed 'Tar Oils') at the top of Frenches Avenue, which later became a scrap metal depot, and the other ran into the Council Yard near the crossing.

Between Dunstable and Leighton Buzzard freight traffic was not heavy, apart from coal for Dunstable Gas Works and chalk from Totternhoe. Both Totternhoe Lime Co. Ltd and Rugby Portland Cement dispatched considerable quantities of chalk from their quarries to Rugby (four train-loads a day up until November 1964).

Being set in a farming belt, Stanbridgeford goods traffic comprised main-

ly cattle, but W.E. Wallace of Eaton Bray sent market garden produce, strawberries and carnations by rail, and, on the receiving side, there was a small
intake of coal.

By far the busiest section of this line was Grovebury Sidings, near Leighton
Buzzard, set in an industrial area surrounded by sand pits. Sand, in early
times, was brought here by horse and cart but an extensive narrow gauge
railway system later took over. Leighton Buzzard stands in an area of good
quality sand, most suitable for glass and ceramics manufacture, and of course
the construction industry. However, the town has not always been in a good
trading position. Before World War I there was only a small profit on sand,
due to foreign competition, especially from Belgium, whose sand was used
as ship ballast and then dumped in this country. Leighton merchants sought
to reduce costs, particularly in transportation but even as late as 1930 foreign
sand was cheaper in the north of England than that from Leighton Buzzard
because of the high cost of rail transport.

Sand was carried from the pits by cart, and later by steam wagons, but
extensive damage was done to the roads in the area and large claims for com-
pensation were made by Bedfordshire County Council. Around 1900 plans
were put forward to provide a railway, thus taking the traffic off the roads,
but nothing materialised. Sand-washing facilities were, however, introduced
at Grovebury Sidings during the 1914-18 War.

Joseph Arnold, a London builders' merchant, had a pit at Leighton in the
mid-19th century, but trade expanded to such an extent that he opened a
depot in Union Street (now Grovebury Road) near to the London & North
Western sidings, where sand was loaded for dispatch, but by 1924 his company had moved to Billington Road.

Garside's first pit was in Billington Road, and a horse-operated railway of
1 ft 7½ in. gauge carried sand to the branch. This pit was worked out by 1916
and quarrying commenced on the other side of the line, where an extensive
2 ft gauge railway was installed. Although the system was not quite complete, the Leighton Buzzard Light Railway was officially opened during the
afternoon of Thursday, 20th November, 1919*.

Grovebury Crossing was not connected to the Leighton Buzzard Light
Railway and so new washing and screening plant was built at Billington
Road, along with a tipping dock beside the sidings. The elevated platform at
the exchange sidings was in use until 1969. It was approached by a double
track extension of the Light Railway and horses controlled shunting operations until 1938-9, when a 20 hp locomotive took over.

Both Arnold's and Garside's had their own standard gauge wagons.
Arnold's had 30 painted in red oxide and Garside's had 48, of which half
were amber and the rest in black livery. · Arnold's were not accepted by

---

* For details of this Light Railway, see *The Leighton Buzzard Light Railway* (new Second
Edition published by The Oakwood Press in 1994).

British Railways at nationalisation, but Garside's had been absorbed into the common pool in 1939. Between 1950 and 1957 British Railways built 1,000 steel 13-ton wagons for the Leighton Buzzard sand traffic.

The Leighton Buzzard Sand Co. Ltd, worked a quarry, Firbank Pit, to the east of Grovebury Crossing. A standard gauge siding ran from near the level crossing right through to the southern edge of the pit. In 1925 this siding was divided into a long loop, with a siding going almost as far as Arnold's pit of 1880. In 1937 part of the loop was lifted so that only two sidings remained. In latter days, following the closure of pits, the sidings were used for storage of British Railways' engineers' wagons. The Leighton Buzzard Brick Co. Ltd opened a pit at Ledburn Road, a mile southwest of Leighton in 1925. To begin with sand was loaded in carts or lorries for transfer to Wing Crossing. Strange as it may seem, much of this sand was carried by rail to Luton builders - via Bedford to Luton Midland sidings!

The German invasion of Belgium in August 1914 cut off supplies of sand, just as the demand for foundry sand by the English munitions factories was rapidly increasing. To avoid the impending crisis, English sources were needed and Leighton Buzzard sand was found to be ideal. Production, therefore, was stepped up and enormous quantities were sent daily by rail and canal to wherever it was needed. Carts and one or two steam tractors hauled the sand from the pits to the railway sidings at Grovebury Crossing and these were soon assisted by 10 more tractors, each hauling five to ten-ton loads, working seven days a week.

Following World War II restrictions on road transport were eased, resulting in less sand being moved by rail. This trend was accelerated by the 17-day strike on British Railways in 1955, when many of Garside's and Arnold's customers sent lorries to collect their sand direct from the quarries. Traffic on the Light Railway fell disastrously and by 1963 only one engine was employed, making three journeys a day. With modernisation of methods British Railways gave the impression they were only interested in full trainloads and as a result traffic to Billington Road dropped to a single train daily.

Grovebury not only dealt with sand but also coal for the Gas Works, owned by the Southern Gas Board, Oxford. Gossard Ltd, clothiers, built a new factory adjacent to the yard in 1921, with a private siding. Other manufacturers which made use of the branch were Cattermole's Blast Grit Ltd, several tile makers and the Grovebury Brickworks, which was taken over by the London Brick Company during World War II and made sand-lime bricks experimentally for a time. Coal and coke was also received at Ledburn Crossing, where in the early days there had been a lime kiln.

It is interesting to note that the Bedfordshire Regional Planning Report of 1937 recommended that every effort be made to encourage the railway company to improve facilities at Dunstable in order to raise them to the same standard as road transport. It was felt that with an improved service to and from London the town of Dunstable might well become an important residential and industrial area. It also recommended that consideration should be give to a connection with the LMS at Luton and the doubling of the line between Luton and Dunstable, together with a new road from Billington Road over the River Ouzel and the canal to join the Wing Road, A418. These proposals were, of course, not implemented at the time. It took some 30 years for the Midland link to be installed and the new road was only recently completed.

Although Luton and Dunstable developed into busy freight handling centres, this was not the case with Luton Hoo. Only small amounts of coal were handled, particularly after the closure of Luton Hoo Gas Works in 1902. Cattle and horses for the Estate made up most of the other goods traffic.

Harpenden (East) was, in its heyday, a very busy little station, handling many kinds of produce and goods. Owen Goldhawk of Kimpton was, for many years, the coal merchant operating from the yard, which received considerable quantities of coal, coke from Luton Gas Works, and anthracite, mainly for Randalls' nurseries. Randalls also received an almost daily consignment of manure from London Zoo, which they collected by horse and cart. 'Rumpus' Grant and Freddie Seaman were in charge of the cart, pulled by a large grey shire horse, during the early 1950s. Produce from the nurseries, including tomatoes, cucumbers and lettuce, was dispatched by rail to Covent Garden, along with watercress from the nearby beds.

About the same time, the Electric Hose and Rubber Company hired Stan Lawrence and his lorry to transport coal from the sidings to its works a short distance away, providing him with almost a full-time job, shovelling loose coal from wagons into his lorry single-handed. Fertilisers brought in by rail were stored in the goods shed before being dispatched to farmers, who also made use of the line for transporting cattle, horses etc.

For a comparatively small station, Wheathampstead handled a fair amount of freight traffic. Extensive nurseries in the area dispatched fresh salad produce in quantity and Harry Batchelor, coal merchant from 1918, received many wagons of coal. His business was taken over by Martells on 1st May, 1957. The arrival of manure at Wheathampstead, again from London Zoo, and its subsequent unloading often brought complaints from the residents of Rose Lane, opposite the sidings.

Due to the fact that Wheathampstead is situated in the midst of agricultural holdings, the railway was frequently used for transporting animals. The cattle pen was removed shortly before closure of the line, so there was no provision for the few animals which arrived thereafter. When two cows arrived early one evening for a farm in Gustard Wood it was decided to unload them onto the station platform and lead them down the steps to a

waiting van. Unfortunately, the twilight and the steps frightened the animals and one ran down the steps and along Codicote Road with the relief
porter still hanging on to its tail. The cow came to a halt some hundred yards
further on, where it was loaded into the van and delivered to its rightful
owner, apparently none the worse for its adventure.

With the arrival of Murphy Chemicals Ltd in 1932 a new form of goods
traffic began. Some of their products were carried in goods vans and part of
the dock at Wheathampstead was covered to protect the packages during
loading. A pipeline was laid from the chemical works to the goods shed to
fill wagons.

Blackbridge gravel pits brought trade to the line for many years. From
1887 excavations were carried out by J. Smart's Gravel Works at Blackbridge
and J.F. Owen's works at Marford - both of which were served by rail connection - Owen's being laid around the turn of the century as the works
extended. The part of Owen's works nearest to Wheathampstead station
soon became exhausted but the area was used again by the Ministry of
Supply during World War II for timber storage, at which time a new siding
was laid. Latterly the area was used as a store for chemical drums but the
siding became overgrown.

Smart's works (later Inns & Co) was by far the largest pit, being 70 ft deep
in places but excavation of gravel virtually ceased by 1948, although a little
was removed for construction of the M1 Motorway. Marford Crossing sidings were out of use shortly after World War II, when the gravel was
exhausted, and by in-filling with refuse the area has been returned to farm-
land. Trains bringing refuse from the London County Council area continued to run, but into Blackbridge siding in order to reclaim those pits. As
already mentioned, these trains used to run through to Harpenden to
reverse, but with the introduction of token working in 1955 a loop was
installed in the dump, saving the journey to Harpenden.

Perhaps the true usefulness of the branch became apparent during the
building of Ebenezer Howard's Garden City (later to become Welwyn
Garden City). At the dawn of construction work there was no station
between Hatfield and Ayot, but in order to facilitate the transportation of
both materials and workmen a temporary wooden platform was built on the
curve at the foot of Ayot Bank, close to the main line, and opened on 16th
August, 1920. Workmen travelled on a specially chartered train from Kings
Cross, running non-stop from Finsbury Park to the new halt. The train then
continued to Ayot to reverse, before returning to Hatfield (probably working
local trains during the day) but picking up the workmen in the evening for
the return journey to London.

On completion of the first phase of the Garden City a new station was built
on the main line, about 200 yards south of the earlier halt, on a site well

known for its wild strawberries. It was opened for passenger use on 20th September, 1926, but the official opening by Mr Neville Chamberlain took place on the 5th October. The new station incorporated platforms for both the Hertford and Dunstable branches.

Originally a farm siding, Horns Siding was taken over in 1920 and extended to provide a delivery point for materials and products needed for the new Garden City, one of the first loads to arrive being kitchen sinks. An extensive narrow gauge railway ran from here, serving the building works and nearby brickworks and sand pits. Latterly used by a coal merchant, it closed in 1962 and was lifted in June 1963.

Ayot handled a varied traffic, ranging from coal to corn. D.F. Payne the local coal and corn merchant had a depot beside the station and Deards' Brickfield (opened in 1866) was sited to the east of the station. Soft red bricks with 'AYOT' moulded into them were produced here and many were carried away by rail. Perhaps the most novel use of this part of the line came just before Christmas, when Father Christmas journeyed from Ayot to Welwyn Garden City on a flat wagon, prior to doing his stint at Welwyn Department Store.

At one time a cattle train departed from Luton at 10 pm every Sunday which called at all the stations to Ayot picking up cattle for Holloway Market on Monday morning. However, as this traffic dwindled a separate train was no longer required and instead a cattle wagon was coupled to the last up passenger train. By 1914 even this had been withdrawn.

During the 1939-45 War the line was very busy and in the immediate post-war period, even busier insofar as freight traffic was concerned. For some time Luton sidings were filled to capacity and wagons bound for Luton had to be stored at Hatfield and other places *en route*. Goods staff worked from the early hours of Sundays sorting out empty wagons to make up a train for Hatfield, to allow an equivalent train of full wagons to come in, and during the week the fastest possible turn-round of wagons had to be achieved.

Between the abolition of Sunday services and about 1960 a special newspaper train left Hatfield in the early hours of Sunday morning, calling at all stations to Luton. The engine returned from Luton at about 8.30 am and travelled light back to Hatfield.

Ayot Bank with its gradient of 1 in 56, and preceeded by a sharp curve, restricted the loads of down trains to 17 loaded wagons and 35 empties, whilst on the up the maximum was 40 wagons for any train, this being the maximum number of wagons the passing loops could accommodate. It was quite common in the steam era for two attempts to be made at climbing the Bank and, on occasions, a banking engine had to be called in to give assistance.

By the 1960s a decline in traffic had set in and at times goods trains were non-existent. The coal traffic had ceased, mainly due to a Concentration Depot being opened adjacent to the Midland main line at Leagrave. Luton Gas Works siding had closed on 31st March, 1965 and Vauxhall Motors no longer needed coal, they had also stopped sending their export vehicles by rail. Nurseries and watercress beds were gradually disappearing and the chemical firms switched to road transport. At Luton the sawmill sidings closed due to the state of the track and eventually all the other private sidings closed.

Ayot sidings were removed and those at Wheathampstead substantially reduced, whilst at Harpenden the sidings were completely taken up and the goods shed demolished. When an engine fell through the sidings at Luton Hoo, due to the rotten state of the sleepers, it was considered better policy to close rather than renew the sidings.

This transformation from capacity-filled sidings to no sidings at all came about in a matter of 20 years, as road transport provided economic alternatives with the advantage of door-to-door cartage, and this rapid decline laid low all hopes of keeping the line running profitably.

Arnold's timber yard near Luton West.   *Authors' Collection*

GNR, 4-4-2T, No. 1550 being prepared for re-railing in May 1926, after its accident.

Authors' Collection

Chapter Six

Accidents and Incidents

As one newspaper of the late 19th century put it, 'It is strange what a number of extraordinary things happen on the Hatfield to Dunstable Branch of the Great Northern Railway'. For such a relatively unimportant line, it certainly had more than its fair share of happenings; some amusing, some extremely unfortunate and some very serious.

As on all lines the weather was to be responsible for some of the disruptions. In fact, one of the earliest recorded accidents was partly caused by snow on the rails. It happened in January 1875 at Dunstable LNWR station when a train owned by that company ran into the back of a stationary Great Northern train.

On Good Friday 1877 snow blocked the line near Luton and at Ayot, closing it for several days. In 1881 a train from Leighton got stuck in the cutting between Dunstable LNWR and Church Street, remaining in the drift until the following day. Passengers had to walk through the snowdrifts into Dunstable. This stretch of line proved to be a considerable hazard in winter, as in 1897 and again in 1900 the cutting was snowed up. In January 1897 the 6 am train, which had not left until 7 am due to the weather, ran into drifts near Blows Down. With the help of all the platelayers in the district, the breakdown gang from Hatfield (it seems a miracle they were able to get there) and about 40 men from London, together with three engines, the train was eventually extricated and arrived in Luton at 12.30 pm. One passenger, Mr Schofield, struggled through the snow to Bute Street carrying the single line staff, since Luton would not let the rescue train into the section without it. Mr Dowse, another passenger, also completed the journey on foot. He was a clerk at the London & County Bank in Luton and had the keys of the branch in his pocket!

In February 1900 the situation was not quite so drastic but again the 6 am train was stuck at Blows Down. Neither this train, nor the 6.25 from Luton could get through but platelayers soon cleared the blockage and the first train arrived at Luton at 7.40 instead of 6.15 am. A week later the line was again blocked and Mr Hills, GNR district superintendent was summoned from London to supervise clearance operations. This achieved, with the help of four engines, the first train arrived at Luton at 2.05 pm, consisting of five coaches packed solid with passengers, who raised loud cheers on arrival at Bute Street.

The last time snow caused chaos was on 19th January, 1963 when a two-coach diesel unit, carrying 25 passengers, ran into a snowdrift between Ayot and Wheathampstead and stuck fast. Efforts were made to dig it out but the

Ayot station building following the devastating fire on 26th July, 1948. This view shows the remains of the down platform booking office and waiting room.   *J. Coe*

Re-railing GNR No. 1550 at Ayot on 8th May, 1926.   *D. White*

wind blew the snow back just as fast as it was dug out. A team of railway-men from Welwyn Garden City made their way across fields to Waterend to rescue the passengers who included an 82-year-old, Mr William Cole. He was carried on a ladder over the fields and arrived in Wheathampstead at about 4.45 pm, four hours late. Meanwhile, some of the other passengers had waded through the snow to Wheathampstead, while the driver, Mr H. Wood of Hatfield, went to Ayot signal box for help. An up goods train was stand-ing at Harpenden awaiting the arrlval of the passenger train and was aban-doned when the line was closed for the night. A diesel locomotive, pushing a steam engine tender as a snow-plough, cleared the line on the following Sunday morning, but the goods train, having frozen up, remained at Harpenden until conditions improved a few days later.

Snow was not the only kind of weather to wreak havoc, as in 1897 the LNWR line at Dunstable was flooded in a storm, as was the cutting under Westfield bridge, Harpenden around 1930. On 4th January, 1898 heavy rain caused a subsidence in the new siding at Brown's timber yard, Luton, and caused the derailment of an engine. During an earlier storm telephone com-munications were put out of order between Dunstable and Stanbridgeford, while at Sewell Bank a driver of a Leighton train noticed a landslide of about 100 tons of earth, which he reported at Dunstable. This was quickly removed and since double track existed at that particular point no major disruption occurred.

To round off the meteorological incidents - wind. On 15th August, 1899 several large poplar trees were blown across the line near Luton Hoo, bring-ing down the telegraph wires. The obstruction was first noticed by the dri-ver of a goods train which, fortunately, managed to stop before running into them. The driver went on foot to Luton Hoo station but because the wires were down no telecommunication could be made, so a porter was dis-patched to the Midland line to inform the Great Northern authorities in Luton. Meanwhile, the goods train shunted back to Luton to fetch the break-down gang, which together, with a gang which had arrived from Hatfield, took an hour to remove the trees. Traffic was restored about 7 pm. Again, during the blizzards of 1916, the wind ripped off the roof of a stand at Luton Football Ground, pitching it onto some carriages which were in an adjacent siding, causing considerable damage.

An incident which could have resulted in serious injury occurred on 11th January, 1930 when a gale forced out glass panes, weighing 56 lb. each, from a verandah on the Luton platform at Welwyn Garden City, and threw them towards the up platforms where people were awaiting the Kings Cross train. Miraculously no-one was hurt.

It was just such a miracle which saved an elderly gentleman by the name of Fletcher who was travelling to Luton Hoo in May 1899 when a stray bul-

Wrestlers Bridge at Hatfield, following its collapse on 20th February, 1962. *Photomatic*

Clearing up after a crash at Welwyn Garden City on 1st June, 1935. The Luton branch disappears to the left under the bridge in the background. *J. Hollingsworth*

let entered his carriage, breaking the window and narrowly missing him.

Damage of a different kind led to a court case brought by Mr Haward, Medical Officer for the GNR, Luton District. On 20th May, 1874 he was travelling with his wife and child in a four-wheeled phaeton. As it approached Hitchin Road bridge at about 2 pm, engine No. 104 (built by Hawthorn & Co. in 1848) let off steam and the horse bolted. The phaeton was smashed to pieces and Mr. Haward seriously injured, with the result that he was away from work for four months. He sued the GNR for £4,000 damages, holding them responsible for the accident. He feared losing his job but was assured in court that he would still be employed - an assertion which, although the case was proved, reduced the financial settlement to £1,150 for him and £250 for his wife.

Horses were, of course, used on and off the railways in the early days and some other incidents have come to light concerning them. Horses were used for shunting and at Wheathampstead there were usually two or three working in the yard. Although this method was quite successful, animals did not have the same control over the situation as present-day shunting engines and on several occasions wagons were allowed to run away through the points out onto the line. On one occasion a wagon got as far as the dip before Leasey Bridge, a distance of about 3/4 mile.

An unfortunate shunting horse came to a nasty end at Luton goods yard in January 1891 when it slipped and fell onto the sharp end of a point lever, which protruded right through its body. The poor animal died minutes later.

The railway companies also owned horse-drawn omnibuses and drays. One such omnibus had arrived at Dunstable station from the Red Lion Hotel on 5th April, 1887 and the busman had gone onto the platform, when the horse started off of its own accord and took the bus back to the Hotel. Later that year a London & North Western drayman was badly hurt when he was thrown from his dray as the horse bolted. This unfortunate tendency caused another incident at Dunstable, this time at Church Street station. On 13th July, 1897, as Mr Deacon's men were unloading some trucks in the goods yard their horse took fright and dashed into one of the carriages of the 11.29 train which was just leaving. The train was brought to a halt until the horse was properly secured and, although considerable damage was done to the cart and carriage, no-one was hurt. No mention was made in the report of any injury to the horse!

Dray horses obviously became accustomed to their routes as in July 1898 a draught horse belonging to the Great Northern Company was observed trotting quietly through the streets of Luton, with its driver 'rattling behind'.

Although company horses were of great use, there were others which caused problems, for instance several strayed onto the line near Luton Hoo in 1894 and delayed trains until they were rounded up and taken to safety.

Not only horses but other animals also strayed onto the line. On 30th September, 1898 a litter of nine piglets managed to squeeze under a fence near Skimpot Lime Works just as a special train came along carrying the Luton Detachment of Volunteers to Dunstable for a funeral. Four of the piglets were killed instantly, and the others were so badly injured they had to be destroyed. This incident reached the London press, who headed the item 'A Train as Sausage Maker'!

In July 1956 the 7.40 am train from Dunstable to Leighton Buzzard was in collision with a cow near the 4 1/2 mile post and in October 1965 several cows strayed onto the track near Wheathampstead where they were run down by a 25-wagon goods train, killing three of them.

Quite a number of incidents took place on the stretch of track between Wheathampstead and Ayot, by far the most disturbing of which occurred on 19th January, 1875. An up goods train, which had left Luton just before the 7.35 pm passenger train, got as far as the incline before Ayot and stalled. It was said afterwards that the engine was old and inefficient. The driver, knowing that the passenger train would soon be due, ran his train backwards for some distance, placed detonators on the line to protect his train and was endeavouring to ascend the incline when the passenger train with a full head of steam rounded the curve and smashed into the disabled goods train. The violence of the collision broke the engine coupling and it rolled down the embankment, turning over twice before the boiler exploded. The driver, Mr J. Payne, had jumped off but the fireman was carried down the bank and seriously injured. Fortunately there were only six passengers on the train, and, although they were cut and bruised, no lives were lost. The wagons of the goods train were smashed to pieces but as soon as possible the injured passengers were taken to Hatfield for medical treatment.

After that incident there was a considerable outcry over the way the train staff system was being worked, by allowing a goods train to depart shortly before a passenger train over the same section.

In contrast, the incident which happened at Ayot during the General Strike of 1926 has an amusing side, although that too could have had disastrous consequences. On 8th May, the Ayot station master was in charge of the signal box and an apprentice driver was handling a goods train of about four wagons bound for Luton. The train approached Ayot and was directed onto the up loop. Unfortunately, both the driver and the station master had overlooked the spring catch points at the other end of the loop. As the train was only proceeding slowly the engine (a 4-4-2T, No. 1550) came to rest tilted over the end of the embankment, high above the road. By mid-day a large crowd of railway strikers had arrived from Hatfield by bicycle to laugh at the 'blackleg' efforts to run the railway!

There were several derailments in the vicinity of Wheathampstead. The earliest seems to have been in 1869 when a driver noticed the points had been left open. He shut off steam and reversed, but had too much speed and went through the points. The engine was derailed, trapping the driver's foot between the engine and tender and seriously injuring the fireman. Fortunately the carriages were kept upright by coming to rest against a horsebox which happened to be in an adjacent siding.

In 1874 the last eight wagons and a brake van became derailed just north of Wheathampstead, ripping up 300 yards of track, and in 1894 a goods train broke in two, the rear part became derailed and the guard suffered from shock. Incidentally, in the same week a gentleman fell from Wheathampstead platform onto the trackbed, cracking two ribs, and was taken to Bute Hospital, Luton for treatment.

Not so lucky was a workman engaged in digging a drain near Wheathampstead in 1914. During the work the poor man (to quote the newspaper report) 'expired'.

Unfortunately, wherever there is a railway there will always be suicides, and this line was no exception. Reports of eight such incidents have been traced and surprisingly two of these were youths aged 15 (at Stanbridgeford) and 16 (near Ayot). The latter carried a note explaining that he had got into bad company and owed £12. One must feel sorry for a platelayer by the name of Rainbow who, whilst walking the line between Dunstable and Luton, found bodies on two consecutive Sundays.

Perhaps one of the earliest trespassing accidents on the branch happened near Luton prior to opening, when the wife of John Francis, a labourer, was crossing the railway fence carrying her husband's dinner. She slipped and fell, breaking a leg in two places. The penalty for taking a short cut over railway lines was paid by a commercial traveller for a straw hat maker, a Mr Griggs, when he was struck by a train about 30 yards from the end of the platform at Bute Street. He was taken to the nearby hospital but died next morning.

Several other passengers came to grief whilst within the bounds of these branch lines. A man was hurt when hit by a carriage door at Bute Street in 1888, but he was able to continue to Leighton Buzzard after treatment. A lady from Wheathampstead died from injuries received when she fell between carriages, again at Bute Street. A gentleman collapsed and died at Dunstable Church Street Station in 1888 after delivering a parcel, and a bricklayer on his way home had just left the train at the same station when he fell down the wooden steps and fractured his skull.

No trace can be found of a passenger fatality in a crash on the line, but there was an accident on the London & North Western section in which passengers had a miraculous escape. It happened on Boxing Day 1873. The 11.05 am from Dunstable had just passed Grovebury Crossing when it left the track and continued upright for some distance until the embankment near the canal bridge, where the first carriage (3rd Class) broke away from the engine, rolled down the bank, overturned and was 'shivered to atoms'. A composite carriage followed, but this landed on its wheels in a ditch. The driver summoned the Leighton station master and permanent way men and released the trapped passengers (20 in all, 8 of whom were injured). The same evening a groom called Wilson was killed by a coal train at Leighton Buzzard as he crossed to the Dunstable platform in the dark.

There were two other fatalities in the Leighton district which illustrate the hazards of working on the railways during those early days. On 31st December, 1868 a gatekeeper at Ledburn Crossing, by the name of Daniel Carpenter, walked in front of a train after giving it the 'all-clear'. At the inquest it came to light that he had been working a 16½ hour day during which he not only manned the crossing, but also assisted with shunting and coal unloading, for which he was paid 17s. 6d. a week. The jury, returning a verdict of 'Accidental Death' due to tiredness added a rider 'that the attention of the London & North Western Railway Company is called to the necessity of limiting the hours worked by their staff to ensure the lives of their passengers'. Surely the lives of their staff should have been considered also! Carpenter was buried in Old Linslade Churchyard the following Sunday, the bearers being railway 'servants' in uniform.

The other accident happened near Wing Road Crossing and concerned Thomas Brown, a goods porter from Nottingham, who had been on loan to Leighton for only a few days when he was wedged between the open door of a wagon and a corn shed (a gap of no more than 4 inches). He was released by his workmates, who had to saw through the woodwork, and taken to University Hospital, London, where he died during that night.

Railway staff working on the track or in goods yards were particularly vulnerable. Reports of several accidents have been found relating to shunting or unloading, together with two fatal accidents to platelayers, and one involving fireman Warner who had occasion to climb on top of the tender, hit his head on a loading gauge and was pitched onto the rails. The engine was immediately stopped and he was extricated from his dangerous position. After treatment for cuts on his face Warner was allowed home to Hatfield.

A combination of tiredness, night-work and heatwave may have led to a fatality to a flagman on duty near Leasey Bridge in 1900. It appears he set his lamp at 'all-clear' and then dozed off whilst still sitting between the rails. The unfortunate man was hit by a goods train from Luton and died two hours later.

Not only people get involved in accidents on railways - crossing gates suffer also, and this line was certainly no exception. Luton Hoo gates seemed to come off worst. In August 1900 a goods train ran past the signals at danger and smashed through the gates and later a car ran down the steep hill and demolished both sets of gates, although much argument ensued as to the condition of the red warning lamps. Leasey Bridge lost its gates twice in a week, the temporary set being shattered by a light engine returning from Luton after working the Sunday morning newspaper train. Stanbridgeford crossing gates were demolished twice in a few weeks in 1935, the second time by a cattle train .

At one of the crossings near Wheathampstead the door of a 1st class carriage came into 'violent collision' with the gate post and was smashed to pieces, glass flying everywhere, but no-one was hurt. An inspector was called in on New Year's Day 1962 following a report from the Luton West signalman that he had seen an open door on a train from Dunstable, but nothing transpired.

Observation played an important part in the life of railway staff, and one can sense the element of surprise with which an engine driver looked back and saw his train of inflammable material rather well alight. This was what happened just north of Luton Hoo in 1897. The driver brought his train to a halt, quickly detached the rear part and hurried off to Luton with the burning wagons in tow, where he stopped beside a hydrant. The Great Northern Fire Brigade dealt with the fire in 20 minutes, but not before considerable damage was done to the wagons and their contents.

From our researches it would appear that wagons and engines have been involved in quite a number of incidents, apart from those already mentioned. The following is a summary:

September 1872 - Broken front axle of engine on 3.30 pm passenger train from Hatfield, 11/2 miles north of New Mill End track ripped up.

August 1877 - Burst tube in engine of passenger train.

October 1888 - Engine of passenger train stuck on points near Dunstable, unable to move backwards or forwards.

November 1888 - LNWR engine derailed during shunting; considerable damage to track.

September 1894 - Engine of last passenger train of day failed at Blows Down, due to broken strap of connecting.rod. Some passengers walked, those who waited arrived at Dunstable just after midnight.

July 1898 - Engine of passenger train derailed in siding at Dunstable.

Just Post War - Shunting engine left line at Luton Gas Works siding. Ended up at the bottom of 15 ft embankment.

1st January 1948 - (First day of Nationalisation) Engine failed at Harpenden East.

June 1948 - Engine derailed at Maple Road Sidings, Luton.

March 1950	-	Ballast wagons pushed so hard against a van in siding at Harpenden East that buffer broke away and van tilted over bank, where it remained for some time.
June 1956	-	Engine forced catch-points in loop at Dunstable North; extensive damage to track.
January 1962	-	Wagons derailed near Luton Yard signal box.
August 1963	-	2 wagons and brake-van derailed at Wheathampstead; dragged through station, still upright. Demolished part of bridge parapet; line closed for two days.
January 1970	-	Train ran through points leading to Maple Road Coal Sidings, Luton. Engine and five wagons left the track, which was torn up.

A derailment with a hint of amusement occurred in March 1898 when a tender left the rails at Luton - and the staff tried to lift it back onto the track. Mighty men they may have been, but not mighty enough, as they eventually had to summon the breakdown gang to put matters right.

By far the most tragic accident happened on 20th April, 1955. The train involved was the 8.30 am push-and-pull from Luton to Dunstable, headed by class '2' 2-6-2 tank, No. 41222, running bunker first, which had just topped the summit of the gradient between Chaul End and Dunstable Town, 10 minutes after leaving Luton, when a fierce blow-back occurred. This forced the enginemen off the footplate, the fireman, Vivien Capp, being fatally injured, whilst the driver, A. Burchett, suffered so badly from shock and burns that it was some time before he could be interviewed. The train, which consisted of two coaches and a fish van, ran on down the gradient for nearly two miles, passing through Dunstable Town and North stations and through the level crossing gates, before it was finally stopped 160 yards beyond the crossing by the guard's vacuum brake.

A less serious accident resulted in the summoning of a steam crane to Harpenden East when the engine of a weedkiller train came to rest between both lines of the loop. The driver had set back before the signal was cleared and services were suspended for some time until the obstruction was removed.

Another engine created havoc in November 1899, this time at Hatfield, when it ran into the Luton train which was awaiting departure. The engine was in the process of removing a horsebox from the end of the Luton train when the driver, being sure he had received a clear signal to go into the sidings, proceeded with considerable force. Six passengers were injured when they were thrown from their seats and many of the carriage windows were shattered.

Accidents on other lines affected the running on the branch lines on several occasions. For example, in February 1921 a St Albans train had arrived at Hatfield, offloaded its passengers and set back so that the engine could change ends. The coaches were pushed out onto the down main line where they hit a goods train, resulting in the derailment of 40 wagons and the coaches (two 6-wheeled and one 8-wheeled). The wreckage blocked the Luton line completely.

Again in January 1957 when an express collided with a local train at Welwyn Garden City all main lines were blocked. Main line services were diverted via Hertford and local services terminated at Hatfield and Welwyn Garden City, with a shuttle service running between the two stations on the Luton line.

The branch was utilised again in 1962 when the Midland main line was blocked by a derailment at Napsbury. Extra trains were laid on between Luton and Hatfield to cope with the London commuters who normally travelled via the Midland line.

Since a section of the branch ran alongside the main line it was only to be expected that if there was a mishap at this point, main line running would also be affected. In fact, this was the case when on 11th January, 1878 a Luton goods train consisting of an engine, tender, two wagons of straw hats and bonnets, ten wagons of coal and a brake van, became derailed due to a broken axle. Before the driver could give a warning the 'Flying Scotsman' came along and, although the vacuum brake was applied, it collided with the wreckage of the goods train. The engine and coaches were thrown across the up main line, the driver being injured and the fireman badly burned, but no passengers were seriously hurt. Shortly afterwards the 8.35 pm passenger train from Peterborough ploughed into the wreckage of both trains. Its engine was over-turned and completely destroyed, resulting in serious injury to both enginemen. A number of passengers were also hurt. At the Inquiry it was said that the newly installed vacuum brake had saved the situation from being much worse.

There were, no doubt, many other incidents and accidents between Hatfield and Dunstable, and Dunstable and Leighton Buzzard. Most of the incidents mentioned here happened in the early days when equipment was basic and the railway age was still settling down. At that time all railway happenings, no matter how trivial, reached the newspapers and, although one cannot believe everything one reads in newspapers, their reports give some idea of conditions in those old company days. Later, when railways became simply a means of communication, much less was written down and it is only through searching, seeing and speaking to those who were there that the later stories have come to light.

Relaying Horns Siding at Welwyn
Garden City in 1920. *D. White*

A GNR dray alongside Messrs A.
Hucklesby and Co.'s Straw Hat and
Plait warehouses, Luton.
Authors' Collection

GNR staff posing for the camera at Luton Bute Street.   *Authors' Collection*

Chapter Seven

Staff

During our research for this book we have come across many reports and reminiscences relating to the staff of the lines. In an effort to bring in a human aspect this chapter is included as a tribute to the men and women who served the branch during its century of operation.

Of course, the position of honour on this, as any railway, was that of station master and although it is impossible to mention them all reference must be made to Henry Vincent Cavill. He became station master at Luton Bute Street in 1870 and remained in that office for 31 years until he collapsed and died suddenly in 1901, aged 60. He was a gentleman of very high esteem, loved and respected by all who worked with him. This fact is borne out by the impressive list of railway-connected mourners, and special note was taken by the local paper reporting his funeral that among the mourners were many staff from the Midland station - a fact which was pleasantly commented on. The bearers were all Great Northern staff, including the goods foreman, draymen, a signalman and a checker.

A man, who was not so well regarded, at any rate by his wife, was the former chief clerk at Harpenden East, Jonas Ellingham. He gained promotion to station master at London Road Station, St Albans, where in August 1918 she attacked him with a heavy railway hammer and battered him to death. He was later described as a 'faithful and zealous official who had worked on the railway since a boy'.

Most of the stations on the branch had their own station master, but when the London Midland took over part of the line those stations came under the control of Midland main line station masters. Harpenden's first station master was George Bendale who came from Dursley, Glos. He was only 28 years old at the time of the appointment and at that time had five children.

One of the pleasant tasks of station masters was to present gifts to railway servants to mark long service or retirement. In October 1889 Mr Cavill presented a 'handsome walnut writing desk, subscribed for by the staff' to T.G. Hearn of Bute Street station, upon his retirement. Since Hearn had joined the company only four years earlier it would appear he was also a well-liked gentleman.

However, there was not always such a convivial atmosphere at Bute Street! At a meeting of goods guards and brakesmen at the Volunteer Tavern on 25th July, 1875 the following resolutions were discussed and unanimously adopted:

1. 60 hours constitute a week's work, ten hours a day, each day's work to stand by

itself, day and night work to be alike.

2. That all time made over ten hours in any one day or night be paid for as overtime at the same rate as other time, namely ten hours for either day or night
work as the case may be.

3. That Sunday work, in all cases, be paid for at the rate of eight hours for a day's
work, Sunday to commence immediately after midnight on Saturday and terminate at midnight of Sunday so that the Sunday of 24 hours be entirely inde-
pendent of any other day.

Unfortunately, we have not been able to find out exactly what their hours
of employment were at the time, but their resolutions were not received too
kindly by the company, who then submitted alternative proposals. At a further meeting of the guards in September 1875 the company's proposals on
pay and hours were rejected and a strike threat was issued. They further
resolved to support financially anyone dismissed for attending the meeting,
until that person could find alternative employment.

Guards, by virtue of their position, needed to be men with initiative and
one who had just that happened to pass through Harpenden East station
when the buildings were receiving a much-needed coat of paint. On arrival
at the station he handed an empty tin to the porter, who had it filled with
paint, and handed it back to the guard when he returned with the next up
train.

One of the regular guards on the branch was a man of small stature, who
earned the name of 'Half-Pint'. One winter as his train made its way down
Ayot Bank it ran into a snowdrift and stuck fast. Undaunted, he took his
shovel and jumped out, with the intention of helping to dig out his train.
Unfortunately the spot at which he chose to alight was a particularly low part
of the bank and he himself disappeared into the drift. His colleagues had to
dig him out before endeavouring to release the train!

It is easy to regard crewmen as just 'the men who worked the trains', but
one of the branch guards was more than that - he had a talent for writing
poetry. The following verses were penned by him:

An Old Ash Tree in Harpenden

I know a tree, a stately Ash, with branches big and tall,
Its roots are tough and strong and deep; It therefore does not fall.
Despite the stress and strain of storms, it proudly rears its head;
'That is a green and lovely tree' so many folks have said.

I watched this tree for many years, as yet it bigger grew,
Its leaves each Autumn tumbled down, each spring they came anew,
And round its trunk the Ivy twined a slender weakling vine.
The Ivy leaves improved its looks and made the tree look fine.

Then when the tree was fully grown the Ivy still would climb
It grew and clung and climbed aloft and covered every limb.
So though the tree would lose its leaves, no more would it look bare
For over every limb and branch the ivy leaves hung there.

I saw that stately tree today, all clothed in lovely green,
With leaves its base and boughs are clad and make a charming scene.
Alas, those leaves are not its own: All Ivy leaves are they
Whilst underneath those clinging vines a skeleton there lay.

There, at its limb-tips, now I see the signs of dire decay -
Poisoned by vines it helped to rear, that tree has passed away.
It still may stand a few years more; its days are numbered though.
It still is clad in living green - a tragic picture now.

How many lives like this great tree were once erect and fine?
Whilst glamorous habits and vices gay around began to twine.
Attractive! Yes! those lives appeared by dazzling vines adorned
Until all virtue sapped away are lives despised and scorned.

Far better be a plain old Ash, without the Ivy frills,
Than be adorned by vines, which slowly surely kills.
Far better live straight, clean and true, a life that's fair to see,
Than live a fast, gay, glamorous life which ends in misery.

There were many long-serving employees, and here we mention just a few.
A platelayer by the name of Arthur French started in 1896 and officially
retired in 1939, but returned as a porter for a while. Another platelayer,
Arthur Bent of Wheathampstead, served for 45 years and then had the mis-
fortune to die on the day of his retirement in July 1949. Harpenden East was
where G. Lord served for 47 years as porter/shunter, also in charge of the
shunting horses.

Another man with a long service record was Stanley Munt of Harpenden
who started as a porter at Wheathampstead and later went to Grimoldby,
Lincs, to train as a signalman. From there he was transferred to London
Road, St Albans and in 1910 back to Wheathampstead, followed by a short
spell at Ayot. In 1926 he became signalman at Harpenden East, where he
remained until his retirement in 1958, at the age of 70. Besides being a signalman he was secretary to the local branch of the National Union of
Railwaymen.

Mr Munt recalled a typical Sunday when he was at Harpenden East. He
would open the signal box early in the morning and then went to service in
the nearby Chapel. He returned to signal the afternoon train and, having
seen it through, left to conduct Sunday School and attend the evening service. To round off his day he went back to the box to allow the cattle train

Luton Goods warehouse with drays loaded with hat boxes, *c.* 1914.   *Luton Museum*

Maurice Munt presenting gifts to station master Mr Lee, on his retirement from Wheathampstead in 1956, after 22 years service.   *Authors' Collection*

through at around 10 pm and then closed up for the night. Work started again for him at around 5 o'clock the next morning. Apart from signalling, he spent many hours cutting the hedges and grass around the station.

The staff, at least during Company days, were very proud of their stations and spent many hours attending to the gardens and generally creating an attractive setting for their passengers. The LNER ran an annual competition between stations and in 1929 Welwyn Garden City were placed 2nd and Luton Hoo 3rd. Welwyn Garden City repeated their success in both 1930 and 1931.

Ayot station was without a water supply, certainly until the 1920s, so they obtained fresh water from Hatfield in an old GNR tender. This stood in the sidings and a porter would fetch supplies from it as and when required, perhaps even taking it to the station master's house behind the station. One of the first station masters at Ayot was a Mr Young, who sported a large white beard.

Bernard Gatward, a porter at Harpenden East until the station closed, could, on cold winter nights, be found in his room building up a fire with several buckets of coal, the heat from which forced one to sit at the other end of the room. He always kept a pitchfork handy to ward off unwelcome visitors!

Female staff were employed on the branch, in fact Wheathampstead had several women in attendance in later years. Two of them, the Misses Chapman emigrated to Australia. Women also helped their husbands with level crossing duties and general station running. Mr & Mrs Cox were responsible for Luton Hoo station and crossing, and it was not unusual for Mrs Cox to be pulling the signals also, although the distant signals caused her something of a problem.

To round off this chapter, mention must be made of Maurice Munt of Harpenden who was for 16 years ticket clerk at Wheathampstead until he was declared 'surplus to requirements' and transferred to Welwyn North. Maurice was a great character and also a great friend and it is to him we owe a great deal of thanks for his co-operation in recalling some of the incidents mentioned in this book. Unfortunately he did not live to see it in print.

AYOT

WELWYN GARDEN CITY

STANBRIDGEFORD

LUTON HOO

CHAUL END

HARPENDEN

WATERLOWS GROUND FRAME

VAUXHALL MOTORS STH FME

LEIGHTON BUZZARD

DUNSTABLE NORTH

These signs and many others items from the line, are on display at Harpenden Railway Museum.

Chapter Eight

After Closure

Dunstable to Leighton Buzzard

The Dunstable North to Leighton Buzzard branch was closed to through goods traffic on 1st January, 1966, but a short length from Grovebury Sidings to Leighton remained open, mainly for sand and fertilizer traffic. Lifting of the track at Dunstable began late in 1968 but, due to the rather halfhearted way in which work proceeded, it took until July 1969 to reach Stanbridgeford. However, all traces of railway equipment were removed, including the ballast, and although the work took a long time a very thorough job resulted. Gowers Siding signal box was sold for preservation to the Leighton Buzzard Narrow Gauge Railway and was removed in January 1969, with the aid of a four-wheeled trolley.

The pretty little country station at Stanbridgeford had to wait until after closure for what was possibly its greatest moment, when, just prior to demolition in October 1968, a forty-strong television crew from Elstree arrived and spent two days filming for 'The Avengers' series.

In December 1968 a plan was put forward to work the section between Grovebury and Leighton Buzzard as a single line, using only the down line, but nothing came of it. The only changes took place at Ledburn Road Crossing, where the road surface was repaired and new gates erected. These gates were opened by train staff as required. It is somewhat ironic that, having carried out this work, British Railways announced its intention to close this section of line. They reckoned that it was losing £26,000 per annum. It was a fact that traffic was on the decline.

Until this time there were two signalman's positions (at Leighton Buzzard shunting frame - the former No. 2 signal box - and at Grovebury Crossing), with a light duty railman at Wing Crossing to handle the two daily trips. This dropped to three trains weekly and later to running as required. From June 1969 trains were run using the 'one engine in steam' principle.

The end came on 5th December 1969 when Brush class '47', No. 1647, performed the 'last rites' by collecting a wagon from Arnold's Siding at Billington Road, from which a condemned container had been delivered the previous day to the Narrow Gauge Railway Society for use as a shed. (It made a spectacular sight when loaded onto a narrow gauge wagon for its journey to Pages Park!)

Lifting work commenced in February 1970 from Stanbridgeford to Billington Road and in October 1970 from Billington Road to Leighton Buzzard, and was completed by February 1971. At Leighton Buzzard the site of the former branch was levelled to form a car park and Wing Crossing and Ledburn Crossing signal boxes were removed to Whipsnade Zoo, to be reinstated on the Umfolozi Railway. By 1975 the trackbed was just a strip of wild land running through the countryside.

A new station was built at Leighton Buzzard and opened in 1991, removing all signs of the former Dunstable branch from that area. Housing development blocked the route at Ledburn and, again in 1991, the Leighton Buzzard by-pass opened which severed the former track bed just east of Stanbridgeford.

The site of Dunstable North station disappeared under an office block.

Hatfield to Dunstable

As soon as commercial working ceased between Luton and Blackbridge all the signal arms were removed, and shortly afterwards two points were lifted from Harpenden East and taken to Luton by train. At Wheathampstead the sidings were cut up and stacked by the line to await removal. Lifting of the actual line commenced at Harpenden East on Sunday, 8th May, 1966, at 3 am - much to the annoyance of local residents! A road crane was used to hoist the rails, which were then conveyed to Luton by locomotive No. D5191. However, only good track was removed - the remainder being cut up on site and taken away by scrap merchants. Lifting proceeded towards Luton, with the crane travelling over any remaining track and removing obstacles in its path as it went - literally! At Luton Hoo it demolished a signal, smashed the lever frame and wrecked the level crossing gates.

On 23rd October, 1966 a special train from Hatfield collected the scrap rails from Wheathampstead sidings, and the section from Harpenden to the down distant signal (London Midland/Eastern boundary) was cut up and removed by scrap merchants starting on 14th January 1967.

The Eastern Region started lifting its track at Harpenden on Sunday 26th February 1967, taking three Sundays to reach Wheathampstead. Problems arose at Wheathampstead as the crane was unable to cross either the river or the road bridges, owing to their shape, resulting in some lengthy diversions by road. Access to the line south of Wheathampstead station was gained through the gravel pits, holes being in-filled with sleepers. As the crane loaded rails from the station area six men and a platform trolley cleared chairs and fishplates from the trackbed north of the road bridge, taking them to the train via the route the crane had taken earlier - a somewhat exhausting occupation. As the wagons were loaded, locomotive No. D5641 took them to Blackbridge Sidings and returned with empties. The points leading into Blackbridge were taken up on Sunday 19th March, 1967 and the line relaid straight into the siding. On completion of this work the crane returned to

Marford Crossing to be taken away by road.

By August 1967 all ballast had been removed between Harpenden and Blackbridge, followed by the Harpenden to Luton Hoo section. The iron deck of the river bridge at Wheathampstead was lifted off on the 3rd August, 1967, and two weeks later Station Road bridge suffered the same fate. A Coles 30-ton crane, perched on the embankment north of the bridge, lifted off the two sides and base, which had first been cut into two, and laid them on the bank for cutting up. Removal began at 9.30 am and was completed two hours later.

While the Council were negotiating purchase of railway land at Wheathampstead in 1968 to provide a by-pass, a 28 day Lease was granted by British Railways to some caravan dwellers who were in the area on a tar laying contract. This move angered local residents, who protested to BR, who in turn assured them that it would not happen again.

Clearance work then stopped, until Sunday 28th July, 1968, when the small bridge at Vauxhall Road, Luton was demolished. This had always been a hazard, particularly in view of the volume of traffic from Vauxhall Motors and in the end that company contributed to its removal to ease traffic flow. Two months later the platform shelter and signal box at Harpenden East were broken up and burnt.

Another year passed before the bridge over the B653 at Luton Hoo was taken apart, on 15th July,1969. The iron deck was lifted off and its side walls cut down to about five feet high. The following Thursday Thrales End Lane bridge at East Hyde was razed to the ground, and during the last week of September both Someries and Watt bridges at Luton Hoo suffered similarly, along with approximately 250 yards of 6 ft high retaining wall.

Blackbridge Sidings closed on 24th May, 1971 and by the 28th June all track between Blackbridge and Ayot had disappeared, most having been taken up by the authorities, but some by scrap merchants. Ayot signal box was burnt down and minor structures demolished at the end of June. Scrap merchants removed the track between Ayot and Digswell Junction cottages at Welwyn Garden City, and the bridge just north of Ayot Station site was removed in July 1971, easing a dangerous bend in the road. Towards the end of that year the cutting was filled in, in readiness for the A1(M) Motorway (then in course of construction) to cross the former railway.

At Welwyn Garden City earthworks were in progress for a new carriage siding complex as part of preparations for the 'Great Northern' Main Line electrification. The connection to the sidings was made by using the former branch line. Meanwhile, at Harpenden the Council had negotiated the purchase of all the former Great Northern land, some of which was later sold off for residential and commercial development. However, in conjunction with a local conservation group, the Council permitted most of the old trackbed

from Westfield Road to Leasey Bridge to be opened as a country walk. The
section between Westfield and Luton Hoo was filled in and levelled.

Turning now to the section between Luton and Dunstable, the station
buildings at both Bute Street and Dunstable North were completely demolished shortly after termination of general freight services, although part of
the track was kept in use for specific traffic. Dunstable Town's wooden platforms and awnings were removed, although the buildings remained for
some time. The yard was utilised for storage of large pipes for oil and gas
pipelines, while the cleared areas at Luton and Dunstable North were adapt-
ed to serve as public car parks. Chaul End signal box, though still in use, was
boarded up and the gatekeeper's house opposite demolished.

Obviously Luton's extensive sidings were no longer required, with the
result that Luton Yard signal box closed on Sunday 25th June, 1967, whereupon the sidings to the goods shed were connected to a ground frame. All
other sidings were taken up and the area adjoining Station Road was levelled
to provide another car park.

In August 1968 trains still served Laporte's Chemical Works and at
Dunstable North the old Great Northern coal yard was made into an oil storage depot served by rail. Between one and three trains daily used these sidings, together with the cement works at Dunstable. Here, coal and empty
wagons were brought into the west triangle, from where the locomotive
would return to the main part of the line and run back to the east triangle to
pick up loaded wagons. Internal shunting was done by diesel locomotives
belonging to the cement company.

During August 1968 all Dunstable North sidings were disconnected from
the signal box. The crossover to the north of the level crossing had been connected to a ground frame and the outer home signal fixed at 'danger', protecting the loop from the Leighton Buzzard section, while on the down line
a sleeper buffer had been erected, topped by a red flag. Engines still used
this part of the line for running round their trains before returning to Luton.

By this time 100-ton oil wagons were beginning to appear and in order to
cater for them, *en route* to Dunstable, about a mile of track near Blows Down
was renewed with heavy duty flat bottom track on concrete sleepers. At the
same time traffic to and from the cement works was increasing, with more
coal going in and about 36 wagons of cement coming out daily. These trains
were later equipped with new wagons capable of holding 40 tons, usually
about 10 wagons at a time. On arrival at Luton the engine was detached and
ran round its train, then propelled it from the old station to the main line,
over the crossing. Much of this cement was dispatched to Birmingham.

In 1969 it was decided to close the section of line from the A5 bridge at
Dunstable, mainly because the bridge had cracked and, due to the lack of
traffic into the Town and North stations, the cost of replacing it was not jus-

tified. The sidings at Dunstable Town were disconnected and the ground frame abolished on 7th March. Dunstable North signal box was closed on Sunday, 23rd March, and demolished soon afterwards. All the track and sidings were lifted and a buffer stop erected just beyond the bridge to give a headshunt to the cement sidings. At the same time a new loop line was installed from Waterlow's siding to the east triangle of the cement works in order to give a run-round. The A5 bridge itself was demolished on Sunday 13th July, 1969 - the Watling Street being closed while the deck was lifted out.

With the closure of Dunstable North signal box the line between Dunstable and Luton West was thereafter worked on the 'one train working' principle, but absolute block working was retained from Luton West to Luton East signal box for a short time. Chaul End box continued to protect the level crossing until 1st November, 1969.

However, these remaining signal boxes were closed on 15th December 1969, resulting in the whole section being worked as a siding, controlled from Luton South signal box on the main line. The East box was converted to serve as a rest room for train crews. The only signals to survive were those protecting the main line connection and fixed distant signals at Luton West and both sides of Chaul End.

At around the same time a catch point was installed adjacent to Bridge No. 36 at Dunstable, in order to prevent wagons from the cement works running away. These points were normally open and the single line token was needed to close them.

During October 1970 contractors were engaged in clearing Gidding's stonemason's yard and the water tower, in order to extend the car park. The old station platforms were removed and the footbridge (which still provided access to the main line station) was extensively repaired. However, in 1975 this footbridge was removed, to be replaced by a new concrete structure. In December 1970 all the fishplates were replaced with heavy duty ones along that part of the line still in use, while redundant sidings were removed and taken away by rail. Luton West signal box was demolished and the whole area tidied up.

By 1971 traffic was again on the decline, mainly because coal for the cement works arrived by road. At this time only around six trains a week left the works, bound for Handsworth, Birmingham - each load comprising approximately 580 tons. Laporte Chemicals stopped using the line towards the end of 1970, and the only other traffic comprised two trains a week to the oil depot and a couple of wagonloads of swarf each week dispatched from Vauxhall Motors. Laporte's siding, which had become heavily rusted, was finally severed from the branch early in 1972. The remaining track and sidings at Bute Street were used as a store for wagons from the main line and during January and February 1971 were filled to capacity with conflat wagons.

In January 1978 a new link road was built between Dunstable Road and New Bedford Road in Luton. To reduce costs, the new bridge needed to carry the railway over the road was built for single track only. By this time insignificant amounts of scrap from Vauxhall, heating oil and cement were being carried and by 1988 there was no trade left on the line - Vauxhall's siding having been lifted in May 1978, the oil depot closed in 1988, along with the cement works.

Although its normal traffic was declining, the branch was included in the schedule of a rail-tour on 17th January 1987, but passengers were not allowed to alight at Dunstable. It then returned to Luton and continued its tour.

When proposals for a new relief road from Luton to Dunstable were put forward it was thought necessary to provide for both rail and road transport running parallel. In fact, it necessitated the taking up of the railway and relaying it to one side of the available land, in order to give sufficient space for the road to be constructed. This done, the new track was connected between Luton West and Chaul End over the weekend of 30th-31st January 1988. Skimpot Lane bridge was replaced and Chaul End level crossing ceased to be, as it was replaced by a bridge. In short a crazy situation arose whereby a new section of railway had been built but by the time it was complete all traffic had ceased.

Meanwhile pressure for a passenger service between Dunstable and Luton had been mounting and there was even a hope at one time that the line could be electrified. A pressure group, A.D.A.P.T. (the Association for Dunstable Area Passenger Trains) was formed, and they ran several special trains from a temporary platform built near Dunstable College, the first of which ran on Sunday 3rd May,1987. Titled 'Dunstabelle I' it journeyed to Brighton, hauled by a class '33' locomotive.

On 8th May, 1988 'Dunstabelle II' went to Portsmouth, again hauled by a class '33' locornotive. On the 30th May, 1988 a shuttle service for Luton and Dunstable carnivals was run, making seven return journies, all full to capacity, again using temporary platforms. This time the motive power was a two-car Cravens DMU, painted green, from Norwich depot.

'Dunstabelle III' to Matlock ran on 30th April, 1989 using a four-car class '101' DMU from Reading Depot, newly painted in Network SouthEast livery. From this day on the line was 'mothballed' - the Department of Transport refusing permission for any more special trains using temporary platforms. A.D.A.P.T. was left to concentrate its campaign on the press, and to lobbying local councils and political parties, some of whom backed the restoration of passenger services, whilst others preferred the line to be withdrawn and a bus-only route provided. Another section of track, south of Luton, between

Kimpton Road bridge and Vauxhall sidings was removed in August 1989 and the land ultimately developed as a retail park.

Although 'mothballed', the line did see one more train along this section and that was a weedkiller train, topped and tailed by class '20' locomotives, which ran in the spring of 1990. At this time there was talk of a new main line station at Luton, to be sited on a large piece of land alongside Crescent Road, which would have allowed direct access to the Dunstable line. However, cash shortages put paid to this idea at the end of 1990 and from then on the branch was allowed to become overgrown.

Early in 1991 BR gave notice of its intention to close the line and its connection with the Midland main line as from 28th March, at which time lifting was to commence, but a re-think was forced upon them because of all the various proposals being made as to the future use of the line, or indeed the land. BR accordingly gave a deadline of 16th December, 1991 for definite proposals to be submitted by interested parties, but none were forthcoming. Accordingly, lifting was authorised and the double track through the former station at Bute Street was lifted in February 1992, but that was as far as it went. At the time of writing track is still *in situ* between Dunstable and approximately Old Bedford Road, Luton and the car park has been extended over part of the area where the track was lifted. Early in 1994 the GNR warehouse was demolished and the site is now being built on.

From the south end of Luton, however, the route of the branch was been designated a public walkway. It is now possible to walk, via Luton Hoo, where the former station house still stands, to Harpenden to meet up with the previously designated walkway between Westfield and Leasey Bridge, but in places where the line has been reclaimed as agricultural land there is no proper pathway to follow.

At Wheathampstead what remains of the station platform is heavily overgrown and the site of the goods yard now has a Club-house built on it. Beyond the by-pass the walkway carries on again to Ayot, where it is known as the Ayot Greenway. The route of the branch still survives through the woods in Welwyn Garden City up to the White Bridge at Digswell Road. Before the bridge, the site of Horn's Siding, so heavily used during the development of the town, now has a leisure complex built on it, known as Campus West. The four old railway cottages remain, though modernised, and their gardens have been extended to take in the area of land once occupied by the trackbed. The keeper's hut from Lyle's Crossing has recently been removed to Harpenden Railway Museum, and completely restored.

And so the history of these branch lines is complete - or is it? Until that last section of track is lifted, or the route blocked by further development in the area of the former Bute Street station, we cannot be sure. With a busy airport and large commuter population, Luton would certainly benefit from a new station. Money was tight when its first station was proposed - but it came about. Who is to say that when the current recession has been overcome Luton should not again welcome passengers from all corners of the railway network - including Dunstable - at a brand new station? Whatever happens, let us not forget those whose dreams and aspirations brought about the original railways. We, who now look back, are indeed grateful to them for their foresight and pioneering spirit. Let us hope that future generations will not hold it against those who, with equal determination, cut short the life and usefulness of these delightful branch lines.

Appendix One

Opening & Closing Dates of Stations

Station or Sidings	Opened for Passengers	Closed For Passengers	Closed For Goods
Hatfield	7th August 1850	-	-
Welwyn Garden City	16th August 1920	20th September 1926	-
New Welwyn Garden City	20th September 1926	-	-
Ayot (Ayot St Peter)	2nd July 1877	26th September 1949	1st May 1963
Wheathampstead	1st September 1860	26th April 1965	26th July 1965
Harpenden (Esat)	1st September 1860	26th April 1965	25th November 1963
New Mill End (Luton Hoo)	1st September 1860	26th April 1965	25th November 1963
Luton (Bute Street)	3rd May 1858	26th April 1965	26th June 1967
Dunstable, Church Street	3rd May 1858	26th April 1965	7th December 1964
Dunstable	1st June 1848	26th April 1965	9th October 1967
Stanbridgeford	Thought to be in use in 1849	2nd July 1962	1st June 1964
Grovebury Sidings	-	-	May 1969
Leighton	9th April 1838	14th February 1859	-
New Leighton	14th February 1859	-	6th February 1967

Renamed Stations

Old Name	New Name	Date
Ayott St Peter	Ayot	April 1878
Harpenden	Harpenden East	25th September 1950
New Mill End	Luton Hoo	1st December 1891
Luton	Luton, Bute Street	25th September 1950
Dunstable, Church Street	Dunstable Town	1st January 1927
Dunstable	Dunstable North	25th September 1950
Leighton	Leighton Buzzard	1st July 1911

Appendix Two

Luton Line Engines
from Hatfield Shed 1924

GNR	LNER	BR	Class	Wheel
1	3001	-	J1	0-6-0
2	3002	-	J1	0-6-0
3	3003	65002	J1	0-6-0
11	3011	-	J1	0-6-0
49	3049	-	D2	4-4-0
101	3101	-	J4	0-6-0
190	3190	69430	N1	0-6-2T
384	3384	-	J3	0-6-0
717	3717	-	J3	0-6-0
745	3745	-	J4	0-6-0
770	3770	-	G1	0-4-4T
1073	4073	-	D3	4-4-0
1078	4078	-	D3	4-4-0
1100	4100	-	J3	0-6-0
1169	4169	-	J3	0-6-0
1377	4377	62177	D2	4-4-0
1534	4534	67385	C12	4-4-2T
1537	4537	67387	C12	4-4-2T
1541	4541	67391	C12	4-4-2T
1548	4548	67398	C12	4-4-2T
1550	4550	-	C12	4-4-2T
1758	4758	69537	N2	0-6-2T
1759	4759	69538	N2	0-6-2T
1760	4760	69539	N2	0-6-2T
1761	4761	69540	N2	0-6-2T
1762	4762	69541	N2	0-6-2T
1763	4763	69542	N2	0-6-2T
1766	4766	69545	N2	0-6-2T
1767	4767	69546	N2	0-6-2T
1770	4770	69549	N2	0-6-2T
GER	LNER	BR	Class	Wheel
993E	7993	69615	N7	0-6-2T
994E	7994	69616	N7	0-6-2T
995E	7995	69617	N7	0-6-2T
*684	3684	-	J57	0-6-0ST

* Hatfield Shunter.

Acknowledgements

Eric Brandreth
Eric Edwards
John Keeling
Keith Ladbury
Rodney Marshall

J. Spencer Gilks
Mike Christensen
John Hinson
Chris Duffell
M. Gulliver

The former staff at BTC Railway Records
Bedford and Hertford County Record Offices
Luton Museum
Local Librarians

and our friends at Digswell, particularly the late Doug White, together
with all those many others who answered letters and advertisements.

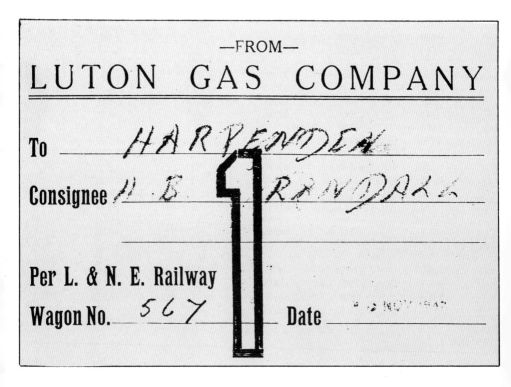

—FROM—

LUTON GAS COMPANY

To _____ *HARPENDEN*

Consignee *H. B.* **1** *RANDALL*

Per L. & N. E. Railway

Wagon No. *567* _____ Date _____

136